> > > > > < < < <

SHADOWS OF TIME

THE GEOLOGY OF BRYCE CANYON NATIONAL PARK

> > > > > < < < <

> > > > > < < < <

> > > > > < < < <

SHADOWS OF TIME

THE GEOLOGY OF BRYCE CANYON NATIONAL PARK

> > > > > < < < < <

TEXT BY FRANK DECOURTEN

> <

PHOTOGRAPHS BY JOHN TELFORD

> <

ILLUSTRATIONS BY HANNAH HINCHMAN

> <

PUBLISHED BY THE BRYCE CANYON NATURAL HISTORY ASSOCIATION, BRYCE CANYON, UTAH 1994

Published by the Bryce Canyon Natural History Association,
a non-profit organization established to aid in the understanding, preservation, and interpretation
of the scenic and historic features of Bryce Canyon National Park.

Text by Frank DeCourten
Photographs ©1994 by John Telford
Illustrations ©1994 by Hannah Hinchman
Design by Lee Riddell
Editing by Heather Bennett
Project coordination by Paula Henrie, Susan Colclazer, and Kent Wintch
Typography includes Charlemagne, Cochin and Univers
Lithography by Paragon Press on Futura Dull Recycled Paper

First Edition
ISBN 1~882054~06~7 SC
ISBN 1~882054~05~9 HC
Library of Congress Catalog Card Number: 94-72234

Photo credits
Page 2: Sunset Point, winter
Page 6: Fairyland Loop Trail
Pages 8 / 9, 10 / 11, 84 / 85: Sunset Point

To order more copies please contact
Bryce Canyon Natural History Association
Bryce Canyon National Park
Bryce Canyon, Utah 84717
Tel 801~834~5322   Fax 801~834~5215

To Amy and Bethany who, like children everywhere,

were born loving Nature.

May the world never steal that from you.

ACKNOWLEDGMENTS

This book is the result of the combined work of a talented and dedicated team. Bryce Canyon Natural History Association and Bryce Canyon National Park saw the need for a new geology book. Susan Colclazer and Paula Henrie provided essential guidance throughout the various stages of work. Past and present Bryce Canyon National Park staff and friends offered helpful comments on the manuscript and were generous in sharing their insights on the region. George Davis, Jeff Eaton, and Gayle Pollock provided valuable comments on the geological substance of the manuscript.

John Telford's photographs both visually explain some of the difficult concepts in the text and inspire us with their sheer majesty. Hannah Hinchman's sensitive drawings illuminate concepts we cannot see. Heather Bennett's thoughtful editing of the raw manuscript insured that non-geologists can understand what is written here. Lee Riddell's design integrated the text, photographs and graphics into this book which I hope captures your imagination and satisfies your interest in geology.

I am grateful to Tom Hill, who served as assistant on numerous field explorations of Bryce Canyon geology. Finally, the DeCourten family deserves credit for their limitless tolerance of the author's numerous absences from home during the course of this project.

Frank DeCourten
Sierra College, California and
Adjunct Curator of Paleontology
Utah Museum of Natural History

CONTENTS

The Geology Of Bryce's Unique Landscapes

PROLOGUE

Bryce Canyon National Park is one of the most photographed landscapes in the world. Everywhere, images of this colorful land are found in books, calendars, posters, and art galleries.

Consequently, first-time visitors to the park usually have some perception of what they will see when they arrive at the top of the escarpment. Despite this indirect familiarity, the reaction of visitors experiencing Bryce for the first time is nearly universal: they are stunned almost into silence by the grandeur and magnificence of the vistas before them. A wave of enchantment engulfs all who struggle to comprehend the magical panorama before them.

The brilliant colors and amazing landforms are unique and seem somehow unbelievable. No printed image of Bryce Canyon National Park can really prepare us for what we see and feel when

> > > > > < < < < <

The reaction of visitors experiencing Bryce for the first time is nearly universal: they are stunned by the grandeur of the vistas before them. No printed image of Bryce Canyon can really prepare us for what we see and feel. Rainbow Point (above). The Sinking Ship and Table Mesa seen from Sunrise Point (left).

> > > > > < < < < <

surrounded by such breathtaking splendor. Imagine what impact this astonishing landscape would have on someone with little idea of what to expect. What would it have been like to explore the Bryce Canyon region over 100 years ago without knowing what you might find?

Imagine traveling on foot or horseback through the forests and meadows, each step leading you closer to the edge of the plateau and the grandeur of the scene below.

What sensations would you have felt as you gazed upon the radiant landscape for the first time? What thoughts would have raced through your mind at the moment the wonderful panorama came into view?

For at least one person, such an experience was not completely imaginary. That person was Clarence E. Dutton.

Rim Trail at sunrise from Inspiration Point (far left).

Sunset at Inspiration Point (left).

CLARENCE DUTTON
AND THE HIGH PLATEAUS OF UTAH

Dutton was the first of many geologists to conduct extensive studies in the region around what is today Bryce Canyon National Park. He spent the summers of 1875, 1876, and 1877 surveying the region and exploring its geologic phenomena under the direction of that legendary figure in the exploration of the West, John Wesley Powell.

The roughly circular province, centered around the Four Corners region, where the modern states of Utah, Colorado, New Mexico, and Arizona join, was named the Colorado Plateau by Powell. Its sweeping vistas of red rock carved into deep canyons, ornate rock spires and monuments, table-like mesas, and pastel painted deserts were virtually uncharted. This desolation charmed Powell and the region became his consuming interest. During his epic exploration of the Colorado River

> > > > > < < < < <

Clarence Dutton was the first of many geologists to conduct extensive studies in the region around what is today Bryce Canyon National Park. He spent the summers of 1875 to 1877 surveying the deep canyons and table-like mesas. Clarence Dutton photo courtesy of the Library of Congress (above). Sunset Point in winter (left).

> > > > > < < < < <

(1869~70), Powell had established the broad outline of the geography and geologic structures of the region. As director of the U.S. Geological Survey in the mid-1870s, he conducted an extensive survey of the Rocky Mountain region. The western and southwestern margin of the Colorado Plateau was particularly intriguing to Powell, because it was one of the least-explored portions of the region and was much different from adjacent land to the west.

What was the nature of the boundary between the Colorado Plateau and the isolated desert mountains lying immediately west? What geologic forces had shaped this boundary and when? Seeking answers to these questions, Powell invited Dutton to lead an expedition to southwest Utah to gather information on the geologic character of this corner of

The scenic Colorado Plateau, centered around the Four Corners region of the American Southwest, is a geological wonderland and home to many national parks.

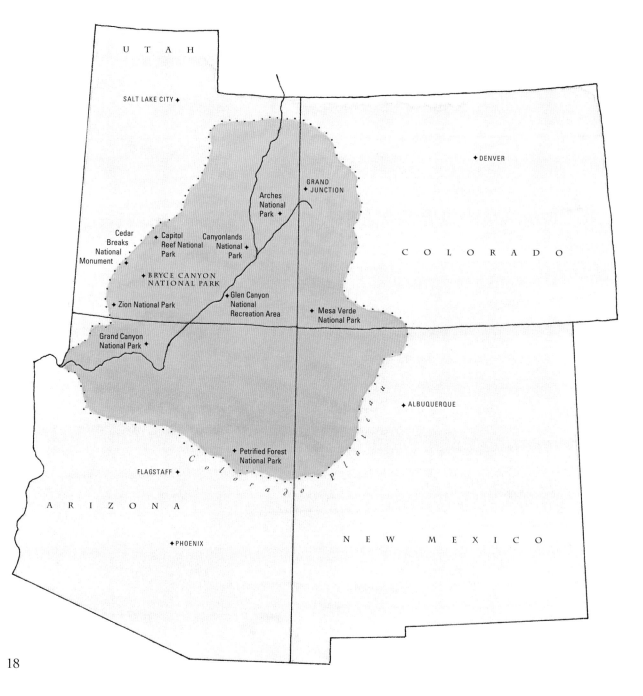

UTAH

SALT LAKE CITY ✦

✦ DENVER

GRAND
JUNCTION ✦

Arches
National
Park ✦

COLORADO

Cedar
Breaks
National
Monument ✦

✦ Capitol
Reef National
Park

Canyonlands
National
Park ✦

✦ BRYCE CANYON
NATIONAL PARK

✦ Glen Canyon
National
Recreation Area

✦ Zion National Park

✦ Mesa Verde
National Park

Grand Canyon
National Park ✦

✦ ALBUQUERQUE

C o l o r a d o   P l a t e a u

✦ Petrified Forest
National Park

FLAGSTAFF ✦

ARIZONA

NEW MEXICO

✦ PHOENIX

the Colorado Plateau. Distrusting his competence as a geologist, Dutton politely refused Powell's initial invitation. But Powell persisted and Dutton finally accepted the mission. Dutton could not have known at the time that he was about to enter a geological wonderland, a region which would attract hundreds of later geologists with its bold exposures of rock recording nature's most fundamental forces and phenomena. In his final report, published in 1880, Dutton outlined the general geologic and geographic patterns of the region, and through his lucid and poetic writing, inspired further investigation in the region which continues even today. No description can surpass Dutton's:

Nature here is more easily read than elsewhere. She seems at times amid those solitudes to have lifted from her countenance the veil of mystery which she habitually wears among the haunts of men . . . The land is stripped of its normal clothing; its cliffs and cañons have dissected it and laid open its tissues and framework, and "he who runs may read," if his eyes have been duly opened.

In Dutton's time, most maps of the Utah region depicted the Wasatch Mountains extending south from near the Idaho-Utah border to the southwestern corner of Utah, forming both the geological backbone of the state and the western edge of the Colorado Plateau province. Dutton discovered, however, that the character of this great mountain system changes dramatically at a point in central Utah near the present-day town of Nephi. The Wasatch Mountains north of this point are generally sharp-crested, with sculpted summits rising to more than 11,000 feet above sea level. The rocks exposed in the Wasatch Mountains are a complex and heterogeneous assemblage, a geological collage battered, torn, and crumpled through a series of mountain-building events beginning more than three billion years ago.

Just east of Nephi, Mt. Nebo forms the southernmost peak on this jagged promontory. South from Mt. Nebo, Dutton discovered that the narrow-crested Wasatch Mountains passed into a series of tablelike plateaus with broad surfaces standing thousands of feet above the land on either side. Three major ranges of plateaus spread south from Mt. Nebo into Arizona, not as a continuous surface, but like rows of rocky slabs laid end to end, separated from each other by linear valleys. The geological substrate of the plateaus contrasts strongly with the tortured tangle of rock seen in the Wasatch Mountains to the north. Layered sedimentary rocks formed from the compaction and cementation of sand, silt, and mud are stacked uniformly beneath the plateaus, broken by fractures or warped by folds only along the margins. Some of the plateaus, particularly the central ones, are capped by lava flows and other volcanic rocks, but the entire assemblage of plateau-forming rock is both younger and less varied than that of the Wasatch Mountains.

Dutton, recognizing the unique nature of this portion of southwestern Utah, established a subdivision of the Colorado Plateau province called the High Plateaus which has been used by geologists and geographers ever since. The title of Dutton's monograph, published in 1880, was *Report on the Geology of the High Plateaus of Utah.*

STEPS AND FINGERS: BROAD STRUCTURE OF THE HIGH PLATEAUS

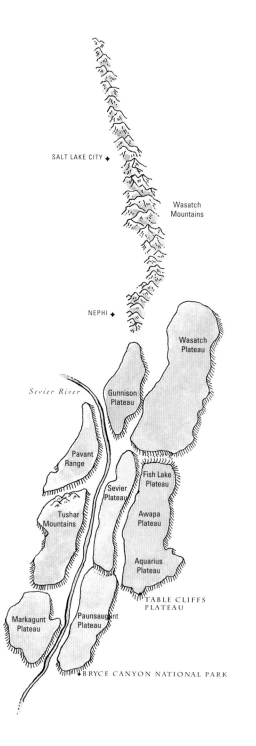

The High Plateaus of Utah form a portion of the western edge of the Colorado Plateau province.

From some distant aerial perspective, such as an orbiting spacecraft or high-altitude airplane, unimaginable in Dutton's time, the three great rows of High Plateaus he named and described can be seen extending south from the Wasatch Mountains like a three-pronged fork. The surfaces of the plateaus, darkened by forests of pine, spruce, and fir stand some 3,000 feet above the less vegetated lowlands and intervening valleys. Named from north to south, the westernmost string of plateaus consists of the Pavant and Tushar mountains, and the Markagunt Plateau. The middle fork of the trident is composed of the Gunnison, Sevier and Paunsaugunt plateaus. The eastern prong of tablelands is less distinct than the others and includes the Wasatch Plateau, the Fish Lake Plateau, the Awapa Plateau, and the Aquarius Plateau with its small southern extension known as the Table Cliffs Plateau.

Each of these three rows of highlands is bounded by great faults. A fault is a fracture in the Earth's crust across which there has been some relative movement of the rocks on either side. Geologists recognize several types of faults, but those which outline the High Plateaus are known as normal faults, the type of rift which can only form by the extension or stretching of the Earth's crust. The relative movement across these faults in the High Plateaus is down on the west and up on the east.

Normal faults are important in controlling the

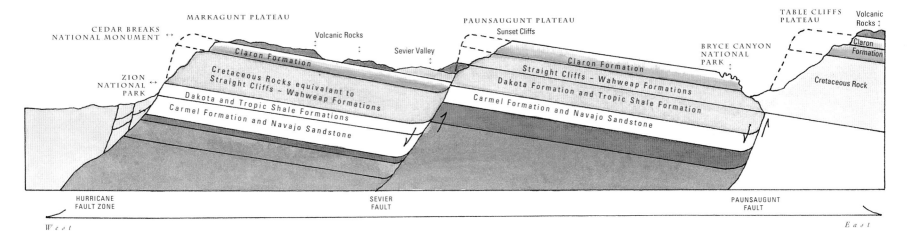

drainage and physiography of High Plateaus and most of the major north-south valleys which separate one row of plateaus from another, have developed along the zones of fracturing. Because of the consistent downward displacement of the western blocks, the plateau surfaces descend from east to west across several faults leading toward the low desert terrain of western Utah. Each of the major faults has been named by geologists. For example the Paunsaugunt Plateau is bounded by the Paunsaugunt Fault on the east, while the Sevier Fault extends along the western margin. Across these bounding faults are the Aquarius Plateau to the northeast and the Markagunt Plateau to the west.

From a high-altitude perspective, you would also notice a series of steps radiating southward from the High Plateaus. This Grand Staircase descends into northern Arizona, where the ground surface begins to rise gently toward the north rim of the Grand Canyon, 8,000 feet above sea level. The long treads of the staircase are tilted gently down to the north and underlain by layers of relatively soft rock, which have been eroded smooth and nearly flat by water, wind, and gravity. The vertical risers are marked by bold south-facing cliffs, where harder rock layers support sheer escarpments.

Each set of cliffs on the Grand Staircase has been christened with a name descriptive of its color. The lowest of the steps rises across the Chocolate Cliffs, the dark-brown eroded edge of 225-million-year-old rocks. To the north above the Chocolate Cliffs, rise the Vermillion Cliffs; their flaming walls of red and brown expose strata (layers of rock) deposited as sand and silt shortly after the first dinosaurs appeared in North America. The White Cliffs are next, a towering wall of sandstone which accumulated in a dune

The plateaus in the Bryce Canyon region are bounded by major normal faults where the eastern blocks have been elevated relative to the western side. The rock layers in each fault-bounded block have been tilted down to the east.

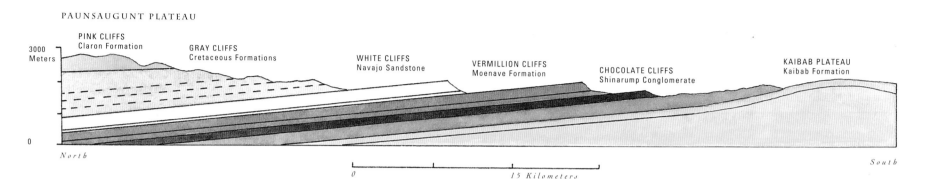

PAUNSAUGUNT PLATEAU

PINK CLIFFS
Claron Formation

GRAY CLIFFS
Cretaceous Formations

WHITE CLIFFS
Navajo Sandstone

VERMILLION CLIFFS
Moenave Formation

CHOCOLATE CLIFFS
Shinarump Conglomerate

KAIBAB PLATEAU
Kaibab Formation

3000
Meters

0

North

0   *15 Kilometers*

South

The cliffs of the Grand Staircase are not the result of faulting. They form through the erosion of a gently tilted sequence of inter-layered hard and soft rock layers. The cliffs mark the eroded edges of the hard layers, while the intervening softer rocks form the "treads" of the staircase.

field of Saharan proportions some 180 million years ago. The Gray Cliffs are the least imposing of the steps in the Grand Staircase, more a sequence of steep hills than true cliffs; they reveal relatively soft siltstone and sandstone deposited along the edge of a shallow sea which covered eastern Utah about 100 million years ago. Finally, and perhaps most vivid of all, the Pink Cliffs define the lofty rims of the southern High Plateaus. The brightly colored limestone and mudstone of the Pink Cliffs originated as soft ooze which accumulated on the floor of a large, erratic lake some 60 million years ago, just after the last of the great dinosaurs disappeared.

The Grand Staircase thus records, layer by layer, over 165 million years of changing landscapes and life in the Colorado Plateau. Like the pages of a book, each layer documents an important chapter in the inconceivably long history of this land. Ascending the Grand Staircase is more than a journey from the low desert to the high forests; it is a trip through unfathomable time. Incredible as it may seem, the rock layers exposed in the Grand Staircase document only a small fraction of the

immense history of our planet. In the depths of the Grand Canyon, erosion along the Colorado River has exposed rocks nearly two billion years old. Even these ancient rocks are less than half as old as the Earth, which evolved from the debris of the sun's birth more than 4.5 billion years ago.

The development of the High Plateaus of Utah took place long after the rock layers exposed along their edges were formed. About 15 million years ago, after a long history of geologic events had produced the layered architecture of the region, the southwestern edge of the Colorado Plateau was broken into a series of blocks by the great stretching forces associated with intense faulting in the Basin and Range province to the west. Great north-south normal faults such as the Sevier and Paunsaugunt faults began to develop at about this time. The blocks of rock isolated by these extensive fractures were elevated in their typical up-to-the-east pattern. The High Plateaus began to emerge as a distinct variation on the general theme of Colorado Plateau geology.

As the individual blocks were displaced upward along the faults, their edges were exposed to the

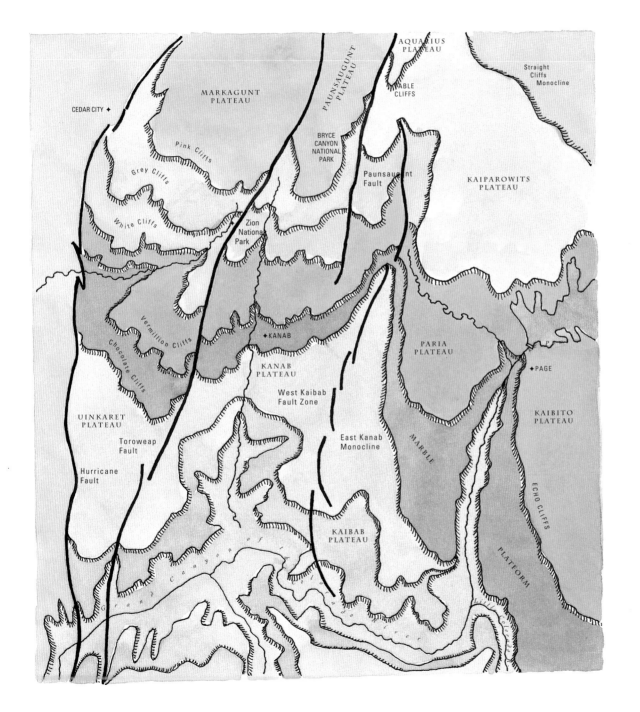

The Grand Staircase descends from the Pink Cliffs in the southern High Plateaus toward the Grand Canyon to the south.

Snowstorm, Sunset Point (far left).

Ponderosa Canyon (left).

ever-present agents of erosion—water, wind, gravity, animal and plant activity, and extremes of temperature. Working in concert with time, these forces attack the fresh exposures of rock, wearing notches into the edges of the plateaus and converting once-solid rock into granular debris. Gullies and canyons notch the rimrock, while erosion of the lower slopes undermines the layers above. Gradually the massive face of the Pink Cliffs has been or is being converted into a spectacular monument to nature's power of erosion. This ravaging process persists today, continually reshaping the face of the land.

25

PAUNSAUGUNT PLATEAU
HOME OF BRYCE CANYON NATIONAL PARK

The Paunsaugunt Plateau, one of the High Plateaus of Utah, is similar in some of its general aspects to the neighboring tablelands. However, it also possesses many distinctive and unique traits which combine to render it an especially fascinating place to learn about a variety of natural phenomena.

The plateau is elongated in a northeast-southwest trend, measuring approximately 30 miles in length and about 12 miles in average width. From a distance, the upper surface of the Paunsaugunt Plateau appears flat, but is actually tilted gently to the northeast. Because of this tilt, the elevation of the surface varies from 9,200 feet on the high southern rim to about 7,800 feet in the northeastern portion. To the west, the plateau is bordered by the Sevier Valley, with an average elevation of 6,500 feet. Tributaries

> > > > > < < < < <

The vigorous erosion along the eastern margin of the Paunsaugunt Plateau has created a magnificently sculpted rim that has been preserved and can be thought of as a moist island rising from the surrounding semi-arid lowlands. Tropic Ditch flash flood (above). Sunrise in the amphitheater from Bryce Point (left).

> > > > > < < < < <

of the north-flowing East Fork of the Sevier River descend the relatively gentle west slope of the plateau, gathering into larger streams to continue flowing northward to the main Sevier River. Ultimately, this water reaches the Sevier (dry) Lake in west-central Utah or is captured by one of several impoundments along the river's course. None of the water flowing off the west slope of the Paunsaugunt Plateau reaches the ocean.

On the east side of the plateau, below the steep escarpment of the Pink Cliffs, the headwaters of the Paria River have carved soft rocks into an uneven basinlike terrain, known as the Tropic Amphitheater, which varies in elevation from 5,800 feet to 6,800 feet. This low and sparsely vegetated area bordering the Paunsaugunt Plateau has been deeply eroded by the many tributaries of the Paria

River, which is itself a branch of the Colorado River drainage system. The vigorous erosion along the eastern margin of the plateau has created a magnificently sculpted rim that has, in part, been preserved within Bryce Canyon National Park. The Paria joins the Colorado at Lee's Ferry in northern Arizona, the point from which many Grand Canyon river trips begin. Eventually, water flowing off the eastern face of the Paunsaugunt Plateau reaches the Pacific Ocean via the Gulf of California, where the Colorado River meets the sea.

The Paunsaugunt Plateau is bounded on the north by the higher Sevier Plateau, which rises to just over 11,000 feet at Mt. Dutton, its highest point. A few miles northwest of Bryce Canyon National Park, the Black Mountains, composed almost entirely of a complex array of relatively young volcanic rocks, mark the boundary between these two high plateaus. To the south, the surface of the Paunsaugunt Plateau terminates at the Pink Cliffs, beyond which the Grand Staircase descends into southern Utah and northern Arizona. So, the east and west boundaries of the Paunsaugunt Plateau are marked by prominent faults, the northern boundary by a step up onto a higher surface across a volcanic mountain range, and the southern margin by the precipitous edge of the Pink Cliffs.

The difference in elevation between the surface of the Paunsaugunt Plateau and the bordering lowlands has a great influence on climate and life in the two areas. Total annual precipitation (rain and snow) on the top of the plateau averages about

16 inches per year. The arid lowlands east of the plateau generally receive less than 10 inches of moisture annually. These climatic differences, coupled with the unique rock types and soils found on and around the plateau, are directly responsible for the distinct plant and animal communities established in the two areas. In most places on the surface of the Paunsaugunt Plateau, dense forests of pine, spruce, and fir support a diverse fauna. In the lower regions bordering the plateau, stands of sagebrush, juniper, pinyon pine, and oakbrush are inhabited by snakes, lizards, rodents, and an array of birds and carnivores quite different from that encountered in the cooler forests above.

Even along the gently sloping top of the Paunsaugunt Plateau, these effects can be witnessed. The higher southern tip, which receives more than 18 inches of precipitation annually is more densely forested than the lower and drier northern extremity. Most of the Paunsaugunt Plateau can thus be thought of as a moist island rising from the surrounding semi-arid lowlands. In the Paiute language, Paunsaugunt means "home of the beaver", a name attesting to the relative abundance of water on this high plateau.

FAULTING AND BLOCKS: GEOLOGIC STRUCTURE OF THE PAUNSAUGUNT PLATEAU

Like most of the adjacent High Plateaus, the Paunsaugunt Plateau was elevated to its lofty heights by faulting which began about 16 million years ago, reached a peak of activity between 5 and

10 million years ago, and has gradually diminished since. Recent geophysical studies have demonstrated that the High Plateaus region is being extended, or stretched, by only about one-hundredth of an inch per year. The rate of extension and the associated intensity of seismic activity was probably much greater in the distant geologic past.

Normal faults bounding the Paunsaugunt Plateau are not simple straight breaks, but large and complex zones of rifting which consist of several faults with more or less uniform trend and form. The Paunsaugunt Fault, for example, extends for at least 70 miles through the eastern foothills of the plateau and has displaced the rock west of it downward by as much as 1,500 feet. The Sevier Fault zone is even more impressive, traceable for over 200 miles from northern Arizona (where it connects with the Toroweap Fault) along the western margin of the Paunsaugunt Plateau, and into the Sevier Valley region farther to the north. The Sevier Fault zone is, in places, several miles wide and the total downward displacement of the western block, which comprises the Markagunt Plateau, exceeds 1,000 feet. The brilliant Sunset Cliffs on the west side of the Paunsaugunt Plateau, which expose the same rock layers seen in Bryce Canyon, have developed from the escarpment heaved upward along the Sevier Fault.

It is important to recognize that the impressive total displacement of blocks bounding the Paunsaugunt and Sevier fault zones represents the cumulative result of millions of years of small-scale slipping along the numerous fractures within each

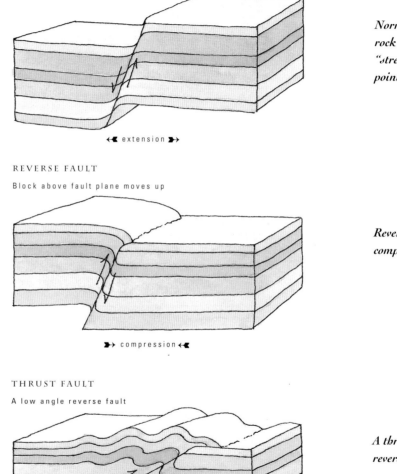

NORMAL FAULT

Block above fault plane moves down

◄ extension ►

REVERSE FAULT

Block above fault plane moves up

► compression ◄

THRUST FAULT

A low angle reverse fault

► compression ◄

Normal faults form when rock is extended or "stretched" to the breaking point.

Reverse faults form by compression of rock.

A thrust fault is a low-angle reverse fault.

Movement of rocks near the Paunsaugunt Fault has resulted in the tilting of otherwise nearly horizontal rock layers in the Bryce Canyon region. Sinking Ship (above) is very near the Paunsaugunt Fault.

zone. Such displacement did not require any catastrophic event. In fact, gradual movement of only about an eighth of an inch per century is all that is required to account for the total offset now observed on the Paunsaugunt Fault. It is true that faults rarely move in such a continuous manner. More commonly, they lie inactive for long periods of time while stress accumulates. When the accumulated stress exceeds a certain level, an earthquake occurs. As the faults on either side of the Paunsaugunt Plateau developed through time, the region was undoubtedly shaken periodically by earthquakes of varying magnitudes.

Though intensity of faulting in the region seems to have diminished in the recent geologic past, some movement has occurred. Lava flows only a few thousand years old were cut by the Sevier Fault along the northwestern side of the Paunsaugunt Plateau. Modern seismic activity in the vicinity of Bryce Canyon however, is slight compared to that in some areas along the western edge of the Colorado Plateau.

In fact, the faults which elevated the Paunsaugunt Plateau are not always easy to observe in the Bryce Canyon region. The sheer escarpment of the plateau is an erosional feature (discussed in a later section), not the result of slip along any fault. The Paunsaugunt Fault actually runs through the lower slopes of the plateau, well east of the rim. Still, the magnitude of the displacement on this fault can be appreciated from points overlooking the splendid eastern vistas. Visitors at Inspiration Point, for example, can stand on white rock layers at an elevation of about

8,100 feet and, looking northeast toward the Table Cliffs and the Aquarius Plateau, see the same white strata exposed at an elevation of nearly 10,000 feet.

To locate the Paunsaugunt Fault, look for places where one type of rock abruptly changes into something different. Along Highway 12, near the Mossy Cave trailhead, the familiar white and pinkish strata can be traced directly eastward into a massive outcrop of gray rocks, in which the strata are poorly layered or not distinct. The steeply inclined line separating these two rock bodies is the trace of the Paunsaugunt Fault. A fault's trace can be defined as the intersection of the fracture with the ground surface.

In this place, movement along the fault has dropped the 50 – 60-million-year-old pink limestone of the western block down against the 85-million-year-old gray rock of the upthrown eastern side. When the blocks on either side of a fault slide past each other, layers of rock close to the fault plane can be warped. As a general rule, the rock layers of the Paunsaugunt Plateau are very gently tilted to the northeast, but in areas near faults, the deformed layers may dip at a steeper angle. When you see such dramatically tilted layers in the Bryce Canyon area, you may suspect a fault nearby. A little further exploration will usually reveal additional evidence of faulting. Sinking Ship, a prominent tilted block visible to the east from most of the viewpoints in the park, is very near the Paunsaugunt Fault. Movement of the blocks adjacent to the fault in that area has jostled the horizontal strata, pitching them up at a relatively high angle.

The Paunsaugunt Fault looks like this where it crosses Highway 12 in the northern part of Bryce Canyon National Park (left). Movement along this fault has dropped younger pink rock down against older gray rock. Above is a close-up of the Paunsaugunt Fault area indicated by the dashed line.

The great normal fault systems observed along the west and east margins of the Paunsaugunt Plateau are the most obvious, but certainly not the only faults developed in the Bryce Canyon region. As the plateau was elevated, stresses within the block led to the development of numerous smaller internal faults. The Fairyland Fault, for example, passes north and south directly under Boat Mesa. The 25-million-year-old caprock of Boat Mesa is not offset by the fault, but the older pink strata below are displaced by about 20 feet across the fault. The Fairyland Fault was probably active much earlier than the Paunsaugunt and Sevier faults and, because it does not exhibit any displacement in the caprock at Boat Mesa, it seems to have ceased activity earlier than the more prominent fractures at the margins of the Paunsaugunt Plateau.

The Peekaboo Fault is another lesser fault which can be observed within the park. It runs through the deep gully just west of Bryce Point and continues south across Yellow Creek basin, east of Paria View. About 40 feet of offset across the Peekaboo Fault can be observed in mismatched layers along the fault. Where the Peekaboo Fault crosses the canyon carved by the headwaters of

Yellow Creek, groundwater rising along the fracture feeds Yellow Spring, a verdant seep on the floor of the canyon. Though their ages and amounts of displacement vary, the Peekaboo and Fairyland faults are both normal faults. Like the Sevier and Paunsaugunt faults, they are caused by the stretching of the crust associated with the formation of the High Plateaus over the past 25 million years.

There are also entirely different kinds of faults in the Paunsaugunt Plateau, structures that are only now beginning to be fully understood by geologists. These faults are called thrust faults because the block above the gently inclined fault plane has moved up relative to the block below it. This relative movement is the opposite of that which defines a normal fault and, more importantly, is generated by a different type of stress. Thrust faults form when rocks are compressed or squeezed rather than extended or stretched. Since different kinds of stress are required to produce normal and thrust faults, it seems that the Bryce Canyon region has experienced at least two distinct phases of faulting.

The most prominent thrust in the Bryce Canyon region is the Ruby's Inn Thrust Fault which passes very near the resort north of the park entrance. The Ruby's Inn Thrust Fault is a major zone of rupture, extending west to east from a point near the mouth of Red Canyon (10 miles west of the park), across the entire width of the northern Paunsaugunt Plateau, and terminating at the Paunsaugunt Fault. Since the thrust is cut by both the Sevier and Paunsaugunt faults, it must have

developed earlier than either of those major normal fault systems. The Ruby's Inn Thrust Fault can be observed in the northern portion of park, where it crosses Highway 12, east of the park boundary. In the south-facing red cliffs at the head of Tropic Canyon, the thrust separates into two parallel strands which extend east to the Paunsaugunt Fault, where they terminate in Little Henderson Canyon.

All along the Ruby's Inn Thrust Fault, blocks of rock have been pushed over underlying strata

The Fairyland Fault on the north side of Boat Mesa (far left). The prominent ledge of light-colored limestone in the middle slope is displaced by the fault, but the caprock is not. This relationship indicates that the Fairyland Fault is not an active rupture and that its movement predates the caprock which is about 30 million years old.

Ruby's Inn Thrust Fault is shown left; the Ruby's Inn Thrust slickenside is shown above.

Hoodoos found just south of Highway 12. The upper gray and tan upper cap of the hoodoos is composed of 90 million year old rock forced along the Ruby's Inn Thrust Fault over the younger pink materials below. The hoodoos represent isolated pillars eroded from the two sheets of rock separated by the thrust fault.

along a surface which descends at a low angle to the north. In the red and pink bluffs north of Highway 12, there are many places where the underside surfaces of overhanging ledges are as smooth as glass, polished and scratched by slip along the fault plane. These surfaces, known as slickenslides, represent the plane of the Ruby's Inn Thrust Fault.

The dislocation of rocks along the Ruby's Inn Thrust Fault has led to the development of a fascinating geological oddity in the seldom-visited northern corner of the park. Because thrust faults are characterized by the upward movement of the block above the fault, older rocks can sometimes be "thrust" up and over younger layers, reversing the normal sequence of younger on older beds.

Just south of the bend in Highway 12 where it begins to descend into Tropic Canyon, several hoodoos stand in a small erosional basin. The hoodoos pale in comparison to the much more abundant and spectacular pillars for which Bryce Canyon National Park is famous, but they have one very unusual aspect. The upper caps of some of these hoodoos in the northern extremity of the park are composed of gray rock about 90 million years old. Below this caprock, the lower portion of the spires consist of the familiar red-pink layers, about 50 million years old. The hoodoos were eroded from a sequence of rock which consisted of a sheet of older rock pushed from the north over the younger materials to the south. The spires standing today in this northern periphery of the park are unique in the fact that they have preserved a small piece of the Ruby's Inn Thrust

Fault, separating the older gray caprock from the younger base of the hoodoos.

As the upper sheet of rock moved south along the Ruby's Inn Thrust Fault, the rock layers above and below were crumpled and deformed. Adjacent to the fault, the layers, originally horizontal, can often be seen inclined at very high angles. In places, they project vertically from the ground. Shattered masses of pink rock are commonly observed along the fault as well. Some of the cracks in the splintered outcrops are filled with white crystalline calcite, formed while water percolated along the open fractures. The movement of the upper sheet of rock along the Ruby's Inn Thrust Fault, accompanied by the folding and crushing of rocks adjacent to the fault, resulted in the shortening of the crust across the zone of deformation. The fracturing and flexing of the rock layers along this fault was sufficient to compress the crust by about 1.5 miles in a north-south direction.

In addition to the Ruby's Inn Thrust Fault, there are other, less prominent compressional faults in the Bryce Canyon region. In the Pine Hills northeast of the park entrance, the Pine Hills Thrust Fault parallels the Ruby's Inn Thrust, except that the upper slab of rock layers has been pushed to the north, not to the south.

Within the main portion of the park, the Bryce Point Fault is northeast-trending and can be traced for about a mile. The Bryce Point Fault plane is inclined at an angle of only about 60 degrees, so it does not qualify as a thrust fault. It is, however, a high-angle reverse fault, with a displacement of about 100 feet, and is a further indication of compressional forces acting in the Bryce Canyon region during the geologic past.

The age and fundamental cause of the thrust faults are problems which geologists are still trying to solve. We do know, however, that the reverse faults represent an early phase of deformation preceding the development of the larger and more prominent normal faults. Long before the beginning of the extension which broke the High Plateaus region into a series of fault-bounded blocks, the area experienced compression, primarily in a north-south direction. The Ruby's Inn and Pine Hills thrust fault systems developed during this time. How old are these faults and when did the compression begin? These are questions which are difficult to answer with precision. Rocks as young as about 50 million years are affected by the thrust faults, so we know that they had to have been active later than that period. Since the thrust faults are cut by normal faults which are generally less than 16 million years old, the compression must have ended before that time.

So, it appears that sometime between about 50 and about 16 million years ago, the Bryce Canyon region was subjected to compressional forces which ultimately ruptured the layered rock and led to the development of the thrust faults.

During this interval of time, the western Colorado Plateau region was affected by two different episodes of geological activity which could have had some role in the thrust faulting. Between 40 and 60 million years ago, most of

western North America was affected by widespread compressional forces, during a period of intense mountain building known as the Laramide Orogeny. In the Colorado Plateau, these forces buckled layered rocks to form such broad uplifts as the San Rafael Swell in central Utah, the Monument Upwarp in the Four Corners region, and the Waterpocket Fold near Capitol Reef National Park. It was also during the Laramide Orogeny that the modern Rocky Mountains in

The east limb of the Bryce Anticline. The rock layers in the middle distance are tilted gently to the east (right side of photo).

ORIGINAL ROCK LAYERS

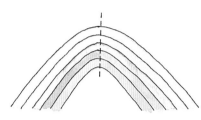

ANTICLINE
Rock layers dip away from center of fold

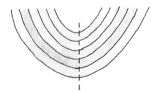

SYNCLINE
Rock layers dip toward center of fold

Compression can lead to the development of folds in rock sequences. An upward fold is called an anticline and a downward fold is called a syncline.

Colorado and the Uinta Mountains in Utah began to rise, yielding to the same forces that were simultaneously warping the strata of the Colorado Plateau. The Ruby's Inn Thrust Fault may be related to the last stage of this orogeny.

Another possible cause of the compression which produced the thrust faults is the intense volcanic activity which began a few miles north of the Paunsaugunt Plateau region about 35 million years ago and continued for another 20 million years. Centered in the Tushar Mountains-Sevier Plateau region to the north, the explosive volcanic eruptions did not directly affect areas as far south as the Paunsaugunt Plateau. However, the movement of great volumes of hot molten rock up through the Earth's crust may have generated compressional stress within the crust which extended beyond the limits of the lava flows and blankets of volcanic ash.

The amount of lava and ash that erupted during this time is staggering; the volcanic rocks in the Marysvale region alone, 50 miles north of Bryce Canyon, are nearly two miles thick and cover over 400 square miles. Placing such a great quantity of molten rock onto the Earth's crust may have generated horizontal compressive stresses sufficient to produce the thrusting.

Quite apart from the thrusting and its causes, there are other geological structures within the park which document an even earlier epoch of compressional deformation. An anticline is a rocky crease from the crest of which layers on either side are inclined downward. The very notion that rocks can be bent or folded seems contrary to our everyday experience. We normally witness the deformation of rock in the fracturing it exhibits when an instantaneous force, such as a blow from a geologist's hammer, is applied. But if a force is applied over a long period of time and under the great pressures that exist deep beneath the Earth's surface, rocks can accommodate the stress by changing their shape instead of by breaking. This is how folds such as anticlines form.

The Bryce Canyon Anticline is a broad fold developed in the older gray rocks exposed below the Pink Cliffs. In the park it is difficult to see because the crest runs in a north-south direction through low hilly terrain east of the rim where the rock exposures are partly obscured by trees and shrubs. Moreover, it is a subtle fold; the descent from its crest is marked by an angle of only a few degrees; and the roughly 95-million-year-old rocks which were subjected to the folding are, for the most part, poorly layered, making it difficult to distinguish their pattern of bending away from the center of the fold. The Bryce Canyon Anticline is, nonetheless, an important structure in influencing the current distribution and thickness of the rocks in question.

The ways in which layers of rock can be formed and later removed are complex. It is important here to understand that some of the drab gray layers of rock deposited during the late Cretaceous Period (around 70 million years ago), were removed by erosion from the crest of the Bryce Canyon Anticline prior to the deposition of the pink, red, and white rimrocks. The upper surface of the gray rock upon which the Pink Cliffs strata

rest represents a surface of erosion known as an unconformity, a gap in the rock record, a period of time when rocks were being removed by erosion. The unconformity at the top of the gray Cretaceous layers, developed above the crest of the Bryce Canyon Anticline, is just one of several such gaps in the sequence of rocks layers at Bryce Canyon National Park. As we will discover, unconformities are important in deciphering the geologic history of the Bryce Canyon region.

In addition to the Bryce Canyon Anticline, there are other examples of folded rock layers within the park. The most obvious is a gentle downward fold, called a syncline, which can be seen by looking northward from Bryce Point. Here, a careful eye can discern the broad downward flexing in the distant pink and gray strata within the Bryce

Amphitheater. Clearly, this nameless syncline was developed after the Bryce Canyon Anticline because it affects the relatively young rimrocks. Though they developed at different times, both the syncline and the Bryce Canyon Anticline are the products of compression. All folds, regardless of their geometry, evince the compression of rock layers.

The book in your hands can prove the point. Try to bend it—upward to make a anticline, downward to make a syncline. What happened to the length while you were folding the book? It decreased as you applied compression to the ends. You can't fold a book by pulling, you have to push it. Rocks can't be folded by being extended, they have to be compressed.

View to the north of the Bryce Syncline. Note that the rock layers on either side dip very gently toward the center.

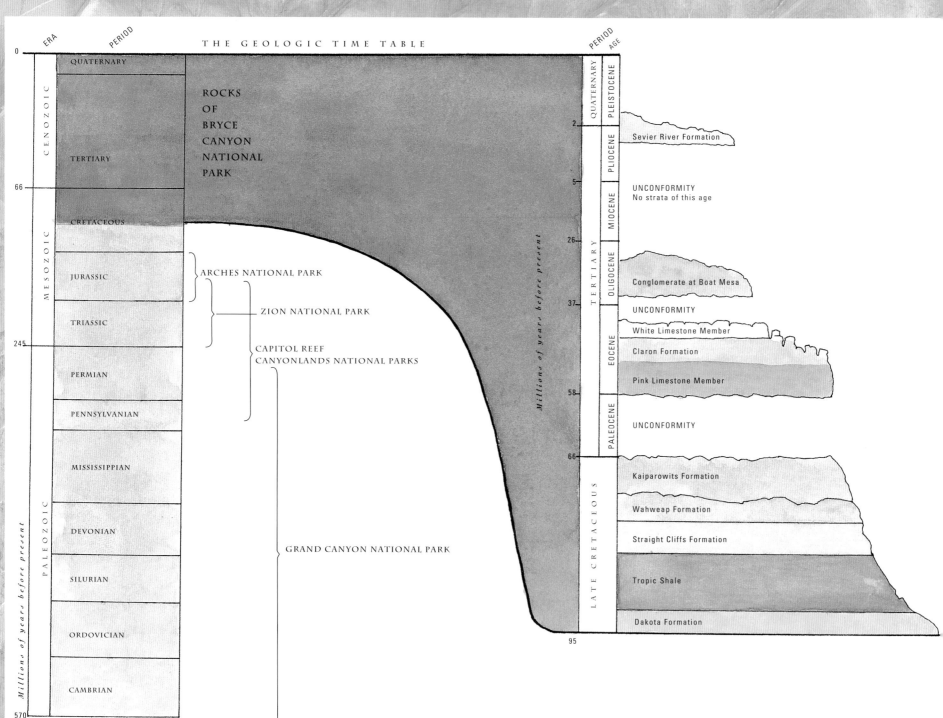

THE GEOLOGIC TIME TABLE

ERA	PERIOD			PERIOD	AGE

ROCKS
OF
BRYCE
CANYON
NATIONAL
PARK

Millions of years before present

Millions of years before present

ERA · PERIOD

0

CENOZOIC

QUATERNARY

TERTIARY

66

MESOZOIC

CRETACEOUS

JURASSIC

TRIASSIC

245

PERMIAN

PENNSYLVANIAN

MISSISSIPPIAN

PALEOZOIC

DEVONIAN

SILURIAN

ORDOVICIAN

CAMBRIAN

570

PRECAMBRIAN
ORIGIN OF EARTH

4600

ARCHES NATIONAL PARK

ZION NATIONAL PARK

CAPITOL REEF
CANYONLANDS NATIONAL PARKS

GRAND CANYON NATIONAL PARK

PERIOD · AGE

0

QUATERNARY — PLEISTOCENE

2

PLIOCENE

Sevier River Formation

5

MIOCENE

UNCONFORMITY
No strata of this age

26

TERTIARY

OLIGOCENE

Conglomerate at Boat Mesa

37

UNCONFORMITY

EOCENE

White Limestone Member

Claron Formation

Pink Limestone Member

58

PALEOCENE

UNCONFORMITY

66

LATE CRETACEOUS

Kaiparowits Formation

Wahweap Formation

Straight Cliffs Formation

Tropic Shale

Dakota Formation

95

ROCKS
PRICELESS CLUES TO THE GEOLOGICAL PAST

Natural wonders abound in the region around Bryce Canyon National Park, but for many visitors it is the rocks exposed in the park which first attract attention. The vibrant colors, the intricate patterns of erosion, and the infinite variations in the surface textures of these rocks are both enchanting and mystifying.

Viewing this wonderland of stone from the rim, or strolling along one of its meandering trails, our curiosity is aroused by the myriad marvels we encounter. We yearn to understand what we see, to deepen our intimacy with this land by comprehending its history. There is no place more effective than Bryce Canyon in stimulating this fundamental human compulsion to know the world around us. And that, in the most basic sense, is what geology is all about.

Geologists employ a three-fold genetic system to classify rocks.

> > > > > < < < < <

We yearn to understand what we see, to deepen our intimacy with this land by comprehending what we see. The eight rock formations of Bryce Canyon National Park are all younger than the strata exposed in other Colorado Plateau parks. Many of the layers are separated by gaps in time known as unconformities. Inspiration Point (above).

> > > > > < < < < <

Rocks with similar features and similar origins are placed in one of three basic categories—igneous, sedimentary, and metamorphic—each of which can be subdivided into smaller groups.

Igneous rocks are those which form from the cooling and solidification of a hot fluid, called magma by geologists. Nearly all magma is generated less than 100 miles beneath the Earth's surface; it does not rise from the much deeper core of the planet. When magma erupts onto the surface in volcanic events, it is called lava. Magma solidifies when the temperature drops below about 600 degrees Centigrade; this cooling may be rapid and obvious, as in the case of volcanic eruptions, or it may proceed slowly in the unseen realm beneath the Earth's surface. The rate of cooling affects the physical characteristics of the resulting

The continuity of sedimentary rock layers at Sunrise Point and other places in Bryce is broken by the intricate patterns of erosion, but horizontal stratification is still obvious from a distance.

rock. Granite, for example, is a "speckled" crystalline igneous rock which represents slowly cooled magma, while even-textured rhyolite is the product of similar magma cooled rapidly during a volcanic eruption. Volcanic rocks may once have covered much of the Bryce Canyon region, but they have been removed by erosion associated with the uplift of the Paunsaugunt Plateau. Igneous rocks, in the form of lava flows and layers of volcanic ash, are found on top of the lower Markagunt Plateau to the west and are particularly widespread to the north in the Sevier Plateau region.

Sedimentary rocks are those which consist of the compacted and cemented products of erosion — pebbles, sand, silt, and other constituents. Sandstone is a common example of sedimentary rock, but not all rocks in this category are granular in character. Limestone, for example, consists of massive calcium carbonate, a mineral precipitated from chemicals dissolved in the water of oceans and lakes. The most distinguishing feature of sedimentary rocks is the layering, or stratification, which they almost always exhibit. The layering in sedimentary rocks may be thick or thin, obscure or distinct, horizontal or tilted, but it is usually apparent to the careful eye. There are a few other rock types such as lava flows (volcanic igneous rocks) which may look layered, but usually a layered rock is a sedimentary rock. The sedimentary rocks are extremely varied, representing materials that accumulated in many different environments including (but not limited to) the floor of the ocean, the bottoms of lakes,

desert dune fields, river channels and floodplains, and coastal settings.

Since sedimentary rocks are the only type which commonly form at the Earth's surface, they provide valuable clues about the environments and life of the ancient past. Because they generally occur in sequences of younger layers stacked on top of older layers, these rocks provide a vertical record of changing conditions through time. As our discussion of general features of the region has already revealed, sedimentary rocks are the dominant type found in Bryce Canyon National Park. We will return to them in the next section.

In the third major category are the metamorphic rocks, those which form from the alteration of older rocks, either igneous or sedimentary, by the combined effects of heat, pressure, and chemically active fluids and vapors in the Earth's crust. Except along fault zones, where the pressures associated with the movement of the blocks on either side have altered the rocks immediately adjacent to the rupture, there are no metamorphic rocks in the Bryce Canyon area.

Implicit in the use of the classification scheme outlined here is the basic assumption that the origin of rocks can be deciphered from their discernable features. After centuries of study, this premise has now been as well substantiated as anything in science can be. Every rock has a history and clues to unraveling it can be found in the details of its composition and texture. Every time you touch a rock, you are touching a historical document. Collecting, elaborate laboratories, or sophisticated analyses are not needed to read the stories of ancient worlds written in stone. A little close examination, coupled with an understanding of the basic features of the various rock types, will allow you to explore landscapes long lost in time.

THE ROCKS OF BRYCE CANYON NATIONAL PARK

All of the rocks forming the eastern edge of the Paunsaugunt Plateau are of the sedimentary type. Geologists employ the concept of a formation in studying such rocks. To many people, a formation is a monolith of stone which has a shape reminiscent of some familiar object—an owl's head, for instance, or a human figure or a covered wagon. To a geologist, however, a formation is a sequence of rock layers which have more or less uniform internal characteristics, and which can be separated from sequences above and below it on the basis of those features. Since a formation consists of layers of rock with nearly uniform features, the entire package of stone most often has had a similar origin. If we think of the individual rock layers as pages in a book, then formations represent whole chapters in the story. A formation generally extends laterally for a considerable distance, but some are exposed in only small areas. Some formations are thousands of feet thick, while others are relatively thin. Most formations are named in reference to the location where they were first defined or are exceptionally well exposed, such as the Sevier River Formation. The word *formation* follows the name, as in the Claron Formation. If the layers within a formation are

composed of nearly identical rock types, a rock name may follow the location epithet, as in the Tropic Shale. The following formations from oldest to youngest, are exposed within the boundaries of Bryce Canyon National Park: the Dakota Formation, the Tropic Shale, the Straight Cliffs Formation, the Wahweap Formation, the Claron Formation, the conglomerate at Boat Mesa, and the Sevier River Formation.

A geological formation is a unit of rock which has more or less uniform characteristics. All of the rocks in this view from Sunrise Point belong in the Claron Formation.

41

The Dakota Formation is exposed in the upper portion of a mesa near the eastern boundary of Bryce Canyon National Park.

The rock layers so boldly exposed in Bryce Canyon National Park are stepping stones to the past, an approximately 100-million-year record of change in life and land of the High Plateaus. Perched high above the surrounding terrain, the strata at Bryce tell of relatively recent events in the geologic story of the Colorado Plateau. Older rocks, documenting more ancient events, are exposed in Zion National Park in the lower Markagunt Plateau to the southwest, and in the Grand Canyon beyond the foot of the Grand Staircase.

THE DAKOTA FORMATION: RECORD OF AN ADVANCING SEA

The succession of rock layers exposed at Bryce begins with the oldest strata which are named the Dakota Formation. Within the park, these rocks can only be seen in the lower Yellow Creek area along the eastern boundary, but the Dakota Formation is widely exposed over an extensive area farther to the east. The Dakota Formation is a heterogeneous (varied or mixed) sequence consisting of interlayered brownish sandstone, fine-grained gray mudstone, crumbly black coal, gray-brown siltstone, and conglomerate (a sedimentary rock composed of rounded pebbles cemented in a sandy matrix which resembles natural concrete).

The Dakota Formation is estimated to be about 95 million years old. This age, established on the basis of the fossils it contains and its correlation with other formations of known age, places its origin in the latter portion of the Cretaceous Period on the geological scale of time. The Dakota is not a thick formation — between 200 and 300 feet in the Bryce Canyon region — but it contains several different kinds of interesting fossils. Impressions of plant leaves and fragments of black carbonized wood, along with the coal, give evidence of abundant vegetation during the time when, and in the environments where, the sediments were deposited. Fossils of vertebrate animals indicate the presence of turtles, lungfish, crocodiles, and small rodentlike primitive mammals. Some of the sandstone and mudstone layers yield fossils of clams and snails similar to those which live in coastal environments today. From this evidence, and the characteristics of the rocks themselves, geologists interpret the Dakota Formation as a record of sediment deposited along a densely forested coastal plain being inundated by a sea advancing from the east.

The Cretaceous was perhaps nature's greatest excursion into mayhem. It was a time when the gradual, steady geologic processes of the planet went haywire. For example, the slow spreading of the ocean basins which results in continental drift was proceeding at a rate up to three times greater than the rate at which such spreading occurs today! During the Cretaceous, the plates of the Earth's brittle crust were dashing around the planet at a geologically reckless speed—as much as 8 inches per year—about five times faster than your fingernails grow. The rapid movement of the plates in the Earth's outer shell is thought to reflect an abrupt change in the circulation of material deep in the interior of our planet.

Partly as a consequence of the high rate of seafloor spreading, great quantities of magma were produced and volcanoes erupted on an unprecedented scale with astonishing intensity. More igneous rock formed worldwide during Cretaceous time than in any other period of geologic history (except perhaps the period just after the formation of the Earth). Ash and gases

erupting from the Cretaceous volcanoes seem to have created a natural "greenhouse effect" which profoundly changed the global climate. It was warm 100 million years ago, very warm. Tropical forests grew as far north as Alaska. The arctic zones disappeared and temperate conditions at the poles caused the icecaps to melt. Water released during this great thaw lifted the world oceans onto the low borderlands of all the Cretaceous continents.

On land and in the swollen seas, a riot of evolution, induced by the rapid and profound environmental changes, produced bizarre life forms: giant seagoing lizards (mosasaurs); flying reptiles the size of a small jet aircraft; the horned, armored, and duck-billed types of dinosaurs (not to mention the fearsome predators, such as Tyrannosaurus, which fed on them); tree-sized ferns and other primitive plants. Finally, there is some good evidence that the Cretaceous might have been punctuated, 66 million years ago, by a collision between the Earth and an asteroid, an appropriately violent end to a turbulent period.

The coal, sandstone, and mudstone of the Dakota Formation accumulated as sediments along the western edge of the Cretaceous Western Interior Seaway which formed when the ancient Gulf of Mexico penetrated north, across the low plains of central North America to join the south-advancing Arctic Ocean. This seaway eventually submerged the entire region where the Rocky Mountains now stand and divided North America into two island continents. The drowning of a coastal plain recorded in the rock layers of the

Fossil leaves and coal in the Dakota Formation provide evidence that the swampy coastal plain of the Cretaceous Period was heavily forested.

The Dakota Formation and the Tropic Shale are exposed in the low, brushy region east of the rim at Bryce Canyon National Park, seen in the far distance in this view from Rainbow Point.

Dakota Formation marks the initial encroachment of the Western Interior Seaway into the Colorado Plateau region. This formation is our link to the beginning of a bizarre chapter in Earth history. Visit one of its outcrops sometime, examine the rocks and fossils you might find, and imagine a world much different from our own.

THE TROPIC SHALE: THE SEA ARRIVES

Resting above the Dakota Formation in the eastern portion of Bryce Canyon National Park is the Tropic Shale. Named for a small town at the base of the eastern escarpment of the Paunsaugunt Plateau, the Tropic Shale consists mostly of soft dark-gray shale, a very fine-grained and even-textured sedimentary rock. Some thin sandstone layers and a few irregular nodules of harder limestone are found associated with the shale in certain horizons within this 700- to 1000-foot-thick formation. Because the soft shale is easily eroded by rain and flowing water, smooth-sided and elaborately gullied hills have developed where the Tropic Shale is exposed in the low foothills, east of and below the rim.

Gray and generally barren, surrounded by the spectacle of the Pink Cliffs, the Tropic Shale badlands seem at first glance to offer little of interest to the naturalist. But, wandering through the brushy gullies cut into the shale, you are likely to find some clues on the origin of the formation. Small coiled shells, somewhat snail-like in their general form, but with ridges and grooves

ornamenting the surface, can often be plucked from the weathered outcrops of the Tropic Shale. These fossils are the most common of several different types of extinct molluscs known as ammonites, primitive relatives of the living squid, octopus, and nautilus. All are (or were) tentacled inhabitants of the sea belonging to the class Cephalopoda.

The fossil ammonites of the Tropic Shale are not the only indication of a marine origin for this rock unit. Recently, the bones of a plesiosaur, a large marine reptile with paddlelike limbs, were discovered in the Tropic Shale outside of the park. The most likely origin for most of the Tropic Shale was a relatively deep, calm sea where only the smallest particles of sediment could be transported from a distant source and deposited on the seafloor. While the first hint of the advance of the Western Interior Seaway is seen in the sedimentary rocks of the Dakota Formation, the Tropic Shale offers clear evidence that by 90 million years ago, the seaway had covered the Paunsaugunt Plateau region completely.

Near its largest stage of development, the Western Interior Seaway extended from central Utah to the region around the present Mississippi River. If the Bryce Canyon region was a seafloor at this time, where was the western shoreline? The geological record of southwestern Utah offers some answers. No late Cretaceous rocks west of the present High Plateaus appear to have been deposited in an open oceanic setting. Sandstone, siltstone, and conglomerate in that region suggest the presence of gravelly streambeds and river floodplains during the time the Tropic Shale was being deposited in the sea to the east.

During the late Cretaceous Period, a vigorous orogeny was underway in what is now western Utah and eastern Nevada. This event is known to geologists as the Sevier Orogeny, named after the Sevier River Valley where the evidence of this upheaval is particularly striking. Great slabs of rock, thousands of feet thick, were broken along low-angle thrust faults and driven from the west to the east, over underlying rock. These thrust faults were similar in form to the Ruby's Inn and Pine Hills thrusts described earlier, but they were larger, developed along a north-south trend, and represent a much earlier phase of mountain building. As the great sheets of rock slowly moved over the material beneath them, they bent, buckled, and cracked until they came to rest as a shattered and contorted mass. New thrust faults periodically developed beneath older ones and the whole stacked sequence would move again. One by one, over millions of years, sheets of tortured rock piled one upon another like the shingles on a roof. This deformation gave rise to the Sevier Orogenic Belt, a prominent mountain system that ran from the southwest corner of Utah north into Idaho and Wyoming.

The Sevier Orogenic Belt must have been an awe-inspiring component of the late-Cretaceous landscape. It was at least 12,000 feet high and densely forested, laced with deep canyons through which swift rivers poured. Its peaks were probably snowcapped much of the year, even in the warm Cretaceous. This mountain chain was also a coastal

mountain range; it formed the barrier beyond which the Western Interior Seaway could not penetrate. The Tropic Shale in the Bryce Canyon area, therefore, probably accumulated in the Western Interior Seaway about 20 miles or so offshore. The foothills of the Sevier Orogenic Belt rose precipitously from this shoreline a few miles farther west.

As the snow melted from the cool summits of the Sevier Orogenic Belt, water trickled down over the fractured and folded bedrock. Descending through steep, boulder-filled gullies, the small rivulets gathered together to form larger brooks. The brooks formed streams and the streams fed rivers, each picking up more and more granular debris. The rivers descended into the Sevier foothills and flowed as turbid braids out across the lowlands, overgrown with jungle.

Entering the sea, they released their loads of sediment grains to the shallow seafloor below. The largest and heaviest particles—sand grains and pebbles—accumulated near the beach, but only the smallest grains could stay in suspension long enough to be transported very far offshore, where they settled as layers of muddy ooze. Occasionally, such ooze buried the coiled shell of an ammonite or the rotting carcass of a plesiosaur, interrupting the decay process and, ultimately, preserving the creatures as fossils.

After millions of years of compaction under thousands of feet of additional sediments, these grains became cemented into an even-textured, gray rock. Uplift of the land followed, and the agents of erosion began to strip away the overlying

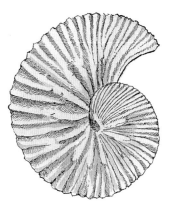

Ammonites Clioscaphites vermiformis (above) are extinct relatives of the modern nautilus Colligniceras woolgari, sp. Collignoniveras (below) and squid. The presence of such fossils in the Tropic Shale is clear evidence of the marine, or oceanic origin of this formation.

Exposures of the Straight Cliffs and Wahweap formations, in the middle distance, are seen from Ponderosa Ridge.

cover. Eventually, the soft gray rock was exposed at the surface where it weathered into low mounds and hills. Behold, the Tropic Shale.

THE STRAIGHT CLIFFS AND WAHWEAP FORMATIONS: THE SEA BEGINS A STAGGERING RETREAT

The next chapter in the geologic history of Bryce Canyon is recorded in the rocks of the Straight Cliffs Formation, and in the Wahweap Formation above it. These rock units were first studied and defined in the Kaiparowits Plateau region east of the Paunsaugunt Plateau, where the distinctive characteristics of each of the two formations are easily observed. In the Bryce Canyon region, however, the differences between these formations are far more subtle. From a distance, both appear as gray and brownish interlayered sandstone and mudstone, of a somewhat lighter tone than the Tropic Shale below. Exposures of the Straight Cliffs and Wahweap formations are commonly covered by debris shed during the erosion of the colorful cliff-forming rimrocks above them.

Where they are exposed, both the Wahweap and Straight Cliffs formations tend to weather into yellowish-gray slopes interrupted in numerous places by ledges and modest cliffs weathered from their harder sandstone layers. Few of the ledge-forming layers extend over a great distance; most are broadly lenticular (thinning at the edges, like a lens) in form and can be traced for only a short distance before they taper out into the finer-grained mudstone which contains them. Patches of shrubs and trees often cover the hillsides and ledges, further obscuring the rocks, so separating the Wahweap from the underlying Straight Cliffs is a challenge, even for many geologists.

To make matters even more confounding, the Wahweap Formation is not always present. Across the axis of the Bryce Canyon Anticline the Wahweap Formation was removed by erosion prior to deposition of the overlying material. In the area around and just south of Paria View, for example, the Wahweap Formation is completely missing and the pink and white caprock of the Paunsaugunt Plateau rests directly on rocks of the Straight Cliffs Formation. Elsewhere, the Wahweap may be only a few feet thick, making it easy to miss if the exposures are hidden by rubble or vegetation.

The Straight Cliffs Formation in the Bryce Canyon area is about 1,300 feet thick and contains a diverse array of interbedded sedimentary rock types. Lenticular layers of gray, brownish, and tan fine-grained sandstone alternate throughout this thick formation with poorly bedded mudstone intervals of gray, charcoal, or purplish color. Some of the sandstone layers contain thin zones of conglomerate composed of varicolored pebbles entombed in a sandy matrix. The dark gray mudstones contain abundant organic material and occasionally produce small pieces of coal. Plant fossils, along with the fragmentary remains of turtles, fish, small dinosaurs, and primitive mammals have also been discovered. East of Bryce Canyon National Park, the Straight Cliffs

Formation contains large amounts of coal formed from the accumulation, compaction, and alteration of the twigs, leaves, and stems of ancient plants.

While some of the lowermost sandstone beds in the Straight Cliffs Formation were deposited as beach sand or in a shallow sea, most of the rocks in the formation appear to have accumulated in coastal swamps, in river channels, or on the floodplains adjacent to river channels. The Straight Cliffs Formation is about 85 million years old.

The Wahweap Formation is up to 700 feet thick in the Bryce Canyon area, but may be much thinner near the axis of the Bryce Canyon Anticline. The Wahweap Formation contains rocks which are similar to those found in the Straight Cliffs Formation, but tends to have fewer thick tan or gray sandstone units and more gritty gray siltstone and purplish-gray mudstone. Most of the rocks of the Wahweap Formation are finer grained, and generally less firmly cemented than those of the Straight Cliffs. For these reasons, the Wahweap exposures are more uniformly smooth sloped, with fewer of the ledges and short cliffs which characterize outcrops of the Straight Cliffs Formation. The Wahweap Formation has produced many interesting (but mostly fragmentary) fossils of dinosaurs, primitive mammals, plants, and invertebrate animals which establish its age at about 80 million years.

The overall similarities of the Wahweap and Straight Cliffs formations suggest a similar origin for the two rock units. The lowermost sandstone layers of the Straight Cliffs were deposited along a beach or perhaps just offshore in a shallow sea.

These first strata, immediately above the open ocean deposits of the Tropic Shale, thus record a receding Western Interior Seaway. The great ocean had begun to retreat and its western shoreline to migrate east.

The mudstone, siltstone, and sandstone in the top layers of the Straight Cliffs-Wahweap interval were all deposited in terrestrial settings such as swamps, lakes, rivers, and floodplains. By about 80 million years ago, the Western Interior Seaway had moved far to the east of the Bryce Canyon region. Near the end of the Cretaceous Period (66 million years ago) the sea drained away completely.

The shrinking of the sea was not uniform and steady; it was a jerky sort of recession, two steps back and one step forward through the last 15 million years or so of the Cretaceous Period. The fine-grained mudstone of the Straight Cliffs-Wahweap sequence documents periods of stagnant water and poor drainage in the region. Each time the shoreline fell away to the east, the rivers still draining the Sevier Orogenic Belt washed sand and silt into the Bryce Canyon region. Then, a brief advance of the shoreline back toward the west would cause the rivers to become sluggish and lead to the development of swampy ponds along the low coast. Over and over these cycles were repeated. The land was alternately swampy, then flushed by vigorous rivers, then swampy again—all in rhythm with the movement of the shoreline.

The gray-brown ledges and slopes of the Straight Cliffs and Wahweap formations conjure up a landscape almost unimaginable from the cool

47

Though the succession of rock layers at Bryce is physically continuous, it is not an unbroken record through time. Unconformities are gaps in the rock sequence. If there is an angular discordance between rock layers above and below the discontinuity, an angular unconformity is recognized.

HOW ANGULAR UNCONFORMITIES FORM

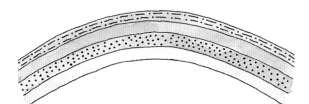

1. DEPOSITION OF ROCK LAYERS

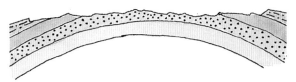

2. FOLDING OF LAYERED SEQUENCE

3. EROSION OF FOLDED ROCKS

UNCONFORMITY

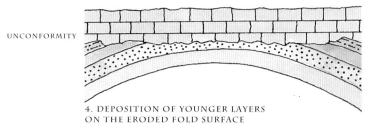

4. DEPOSITION OF YOUNGER LAYERS ON THE ERODED FOLD SURFACE

canyons of today's high plateaus: a coastal lowland, across which rivers flow east to meet the sea; a dense jungle of primitive plants alive with the throaty hisses of dinosaurs and the buzz of insects; furry rodentlike mammals warming themselves under the tropical sun; steamy air hanging above blackwater swamps teeming with turtles. This ancient world has been recorded in stone.

THE CRETACEOUS-TERTIARY UNCONFORMITY: A MISSING CHAPTER

After the deposition of the Wahweap Formation, around 80 million years ago, additional sediment of the same general type probably continued to accumulate until the end of the Cretaceous Period, and even into the earliest part of the succeeding Tertiary Period. In and around the Tropic Amphitheater east of the park, several additional formations above the Wahweap have been defined by geologists. The Kaiparowits Formation, the Canaan Peak Formation, and the Pine Hollow Formation are examples of such units. However, no rocks of this age can be identified with certainty in Bryce Canyon National Park. They were probably present at one time, but eroded away from the Bryce Canyon Anticline before the younger materials in the rimrocks were deposited.

Geologists cannot be sure exactly when the Bryce Canyon Anticline developed, but it must have happened between 50 and 80 million years ago. These constraints on the age of the folding stem from two simple observations. The Wahweap

Formation is the youngest rock unit involved in the folding, therefore the fold must postdate it. The younger rocks of the Pink Cliffs are deposited on the surface eroded across the top of the fold and are not warped over its crest; therefore, those strata must have accumulated after the folding.

A good guess is that the Bryce Canyon Anticline developed during the earliest Tertiary Period in response to the widespread disturbances known collectively as the Laramide Orogeny, discussed earlier. As the anticline bulged upward, the Cretaceous rocks along its crest were eroded off. Several thousand feet of post-Wahweap sedimentary rocks may have been removed during this time. Eventually, a flat surface of erosion formed across the beveled axis of the anticline. It was upon this eroded surface that the horizontal layers of the pink Claron Formation accumulated. The surface which separates the gray and brown Cretaceous strata from the colorful strata above is therefore an unconformity—a break in the rock record which corresponds to the time of development and erosion of the Bryce Canyon Anticline.

The uppermost layers of the Wahweap Formation can, in places, be seen to terminate against the pink bottom beds of the Claron Formation at a slight angle. Such a juncture of rock layers is known as an angular unconformity. This angular unconformity hides 30 million years of history in the Bryce Canyon region. Aside from the growth and erosion of the Bryce Canyon Anticline, we can say little about the events which took place during this interval, because we have no

rocks to "read." When the geologic story resumes, 50 – 60 million years ago, we find conditions quite different from those which prevailed during the late Cretaceous Period.

Along the Queen's Garden Trail, the Claron Formation exhibits the variety of its pastel hues.

THE CLARON FORMATION: RADIANT RECORD OF A GREAT LAKE

Many visitors to Bryce Canyon National Park regard the multihued cliffs along the rim, eroded into picturesque columns and pillars, as highlights

of the region. Indeed, the astonishing colors and shapes of these rocks, and the ever-changing play of shadow and light upon them, cast an enchanting spell. From the geological perspective they are equally appealing. Beneath the magnificent beauty of their exterior, these rocks chronicle, in the details of their composition, texture, and layering, an extraordinary series of events in the early Tertiary Period. These are the rocks of the Claron Formation.

The Claron Formation is informally divided by geologists into two parts, called members, which are easy to identify because they are based primarily on color, a quality which is more obvious to most people than the finer details of rock composition or texture.

The pink member of the Claron is the lowermost of the two components and consists mostly of pale pink, lavender, or red limestone and mudstone, with a few beds of sandstone shuffled sporadically into the sequence. It is between 500 and 700 feet thick in the park and is the rock unit from which nearly all of the spectacular hoodoos and badlands have developed.

The limestone in the pink member tends to be impure, containing abundant silt and clay. The mudstone is normally present in relatively thin layers between thicker limestone beds. Near the base of the pink member, a coarse conglomerate is often found which contains pebbles (up to about two inches in size) and cobbles (larger than about two inches in size) of black, white, and red rock, embedded in a sandy matrix. Most of the limestone in the pink member is composed of the mineral

calcite (calcium carbonate), but some layers have dolomite (calcium-magnesium carbonate) as well. Both calcite and dolomite are soluble minerals (that is, they dissolve in water). Dolomite is less soluble than calcite, however, so the dolomitic limestone layers often protrude over recesses eroded into the more vulnerable limestone beds.

The kaleidoscopic colors of the pink member are the result of small amounts of iron or manganese combined in varying ratios with oxygen. Such

The white limestone member of the Claron Formation is particularly prominent at Rainbow Point (left), where it may be up to 300 feet thick.

The varying colors and rock types in the Claron Formation (above) combine to create a wonderland.

White-capped hoodoos can be seen at the head of Agua Canyon. Resistant limestone forms the upper portion of the hoodoos.

combinations between metallic elements and oxygen are known as oxide minerals. There are several different color-producing oxides present as impurities in the rocks of the pink member. Small amounts of different iron oxides in the limestone and mudstone may produce a red, yellow, or brown color. Manganese oxides, on the other hand, impart to the rock a hue of purple, pale blue, or lavender.

South of Sunset Point, you may notice that the pink rimrocks at Bryce are capped by approximately 300 feet of white strata. These thick layers of relatively pure limestone, light gray to creamy white in color, associated with only a few thin beds of gray mudstone, belong to the white member of the Claron Formation. The limestone of the white member is not as distinctly layered as the rocks of the pink member and is associated with much less mudstone and no sandstone. The white member is also fairly uniform in composition. It generally erodes to form sheer cliffs above the spires and hoodoos carved into the more varied pink layers.

North of Sunset Point, the white member has been completely eroded from the surface of the Paunsaugunt Plateau. In this area, the pink member forms the rimrock. Even to the south, the white member is present only in patches, but is particularly prominent as the brilliant caprock at Bryce Point, in the vicinity of Farview Point, and at Yovimpa and Rainbow Points.

Prior to the late 1960s, the Claron Formation was known to most geologists as the Wasatch Formation. Older literature on the geology of the Bryce Canyon area still describes the Claron Formation under that name. Still other geologists have called these strata the "Cedar Breaks Formation" or "Bryce Canyon beds."

Why so much historic uncertainty about the proper name to apply to the Claron? The answer demands consideration of what a geological formation is, and an appreciation of some of the unique qualities of the Claron Formation which limit our understanding of its age and origin.

Remember that a formation, to the geologist, is a blanket of rock with more or less uniform internal characteristics serving to separate it from other rock units. In addition, a formation should be thick enough and sufficiently extensive to be traced (or mapped) over a reasonably large area. New formations are never established on the basis of a single outcrop or an individual thin layer of a given rock type. Though all formations have some lateral continuity (from a few square miles to hundreds of thousands of square miles), none can be traced forever. They all terminate somewhere, usually at the limits of the ancient basin in which they accumulated.

For example, if we envision a hypothetical formation which consists of sandstone deposited by wind in the form of dunes, it can be no more extensive than the original dune field. Beyond the edges of the ancient dunes, there may have been other sandstones forming, perhaps deposited by rivers, in lakes, or in the ocean. These adjacent sandstones would likely differ in terms of grain size, style of layering, and composition, owing to their different origins. River-deposited sandstone and dune-deposited sandstone would probably not be assigned to the same formation because they would have different attributes, even though they may have accumulated at the same time and in neighboring localities. The rocks in some formations do change, in exactly this manner, as they are traced along from one place to another, from one environment of deposition to another. More commonly, however, exposures of the original blanket of sedimentary rocks are interrupted by later erosion so that outcrops become isolated and cannot be physically correlated over a broad area. The tendency,

therefore, is for geologists to apply different formation names to two sequences of rock when their characteristics are sufficiently different, even if they share some characteristics in common.

Now, let us return to the problem of what to call the white and pink rimrocks at Bryce. The Wasatch Formation was defined by pioneer geologists in the late 1860s in southwestern Wyoming and northern Utah. In that area, the term was applied to layers of sandstone and conglomerate of early Tertiary age, shed from the rising Uinta and Wasatch mountains. As geological exploration of the Rocky Mountain region continued through the latter part of the nineteenth century, the name Wasatch Formation was extended into other areas.

Because of the mountain building that was in progress during the early part of the Tertiary Period, strata of this age in the Utah region tend to be rather complex assemblages of mixed rock types, derived from a variety of different sources. Lacking any precise definition of its constituent rocks, the name Wasatch Formation came to be applied to virtually any sequence of coarse-grained sedimentary rock deposited during the early Tertiary. Rocks in the Bryce Canyon region were attributed to the Wasatch Formation in 1909, even though Dutton had called the same beds "the Pink Cliff series" in 1880.

The name stuck until the late 1960s when geologists, realizing that these pink rocks were dominantly limestones (not sandstones), and were deposited in a much different setting and perhaps at a different time than the "Wasatch," sought a

The remains of aquatic snails such as __Physa peromatis__ are not abundant in the Claron Formation, but help confirm that these sediments were deposited in an ancient lake system.

53

Uneven layering in the limestone of the Claron Formation seen along the Peekaboo Trail (above).

A ledge of red sandstone in the Claron Formation is exposed near Rainbow Point (right).

The lake basin system of the early Tertiary Period in the Colorado Plateau is illustrated to the right. During dry intervals, the lake would contract and possibly separate into several isolated lakes. The lakes may have been connected during wet intervals (far right).

more appropriate name for the pink cliffs. The term Claron Formation had been used for a similar sequence of rocks in the Iron Springs area just west of the High Plateaus in 1908. That name was officially recorded with the USGS and is now used.

Uncertainty persists, even today, over the precise age and origin of these rocks. Limestone, the most abundant type of rock in the Claron, generally forms in bodies of standing water such as lakes or oceans. The sandstones and conglomerates interbedded with the limestones in the Claron Formation almost certainly represent materials deposited by streams entering such a body of water. Geologists generally agree that most of the Claron Formation represents sediment deposited in a large system of ancient lakes stretching through central Utah from the Bryce Canyon region north to the Uinta Mountains.

In order to establish a precise origin for these strata, geologists must examine the fine details of the layering, the fossils, and the composition and arrangement of constituent grains. But the rocks of the Claron Formation do not yield their secrets easily. They seem to have been altered by some processes which have obliterated or obscured most of their primary features.

The fine details of the layering, a fundamental property of sedimentary rocks, are indistinct and irregular when examined on a small scale. Looking closely at an exposure of the Claron, you will see little detail in the texture—a bit of mottling perhaps, some small discolored patches here and there, a few faint wispy lines of stratification—but nothing that stands out clearly. Fossils? They are known to occur in the Claron, but they are rare, almost always rather poorly preserved, and not especially diagnostic of age or environment. The meager fossil evidence—mostly remains of freshwater snails and clams—does, however, support the inference of a lakebed origin.

Sandstone layers interspersed through the Claron Formation, particularly in the pink member, probably represent dry intervals in the history of the Tertiary lake system. Losing more water through evaporation than they received from inflow, the lakes would contract during such arid cycles, while rivers washed sand and pebbles over muddy limestone sediments. Eventually, the drought would pass and the lakes would expand again, at times developing a single large lake from several smaller ones. Rising water would cover the sandy sediment which had been swept into the basins during their low stages. New layers of limestone or mudstone would begin to form. Over millions of years, the repetitive episodes of expansion and recession generated a varied mixture of layered rocks. Though it is not yet possible to define precisely the number and duration of such lake cycles, the Claron Formation appears to have been born of a capricious parent.

But take a step back and consider geological events on a broader scale. 120 miles north of the Paunsaugunt Plateau, in the Wasatch Plateau region, rocks that are roughly the same age as the Claron Formation are known as the Flagstaff Formation. Like the Claron, the Flagstaff Formation consists of limestone, shale, and mudstone. The limestone of the Flagstaff, though, is composed almost entirely of calcite with only tiny amounts of silt and clay mixed through it. There is no sandstone or conglomerate in the Flagstaff sediments, and mudstone makes up only a small fraction of the formation. In addition, the primary structures of the Flagstaff Formation are very well preserved; fossil fish and molluscs, spherical structures built by algae, fine laminations, and distinct layering are all typical.

For these reasons, the Flagstaff is thought to represent sediment which accumulated in the deepest and largest of the several ancient lake basins, where more permanent submersion, deeper water, and minimal influx of silt and sand would have occurred.

Because exposures of these ancient lake beds are not continuous throughout the High Plateaus, the Flagstaff Formation cannot be matched physically with the Claron Formation. It is very likely, nonetheless, that these two formations

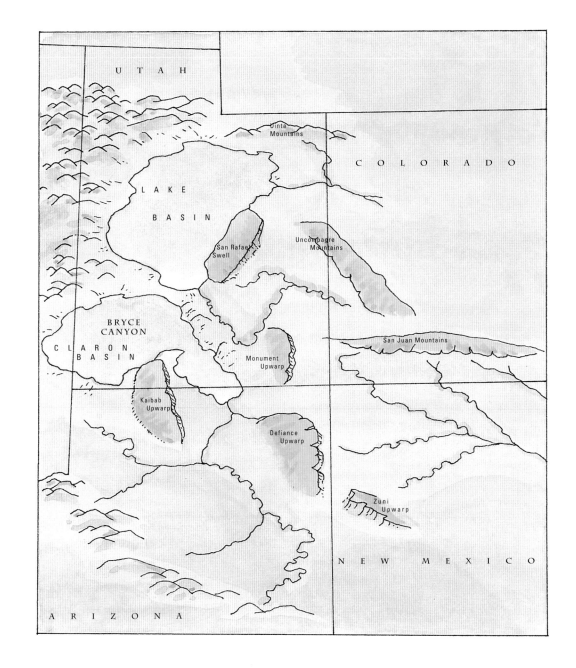

accumulated in the same system of lakes during the early Tertiary Period.

However, the Claron Formation formed in the southernmost basin of the lake system, where the water was very shallow. The bottom of this narrow basin, enclosed on three sides, would be more likely to have been exposed during the low-water stages than the more deeply submerged larger basins to the north. During arid periods, sandy and muddy sediment transported by rivers would be deposited on the exposed beds around the edge of the more isolated basins, while limestone and shale continued to accumulate in the larger lakes.

If we accept this geologic evidence of the conditions under which the Claron Formation was deposited, then a plausible cause for the shrouded layering and textural features becomes apparent. During times of falling water, the shallow lake bottom would have been exposed. Water penetrating down through the mantle of soil on the emergent surface may have dissolved some of the minerals, leaving others behind. Plants rooting in the soil, and perhaps even animals digging through it, might have obscured the finer details of the original layering.

This theory—that the obliteration of primary features in these rocks is the result of pedogenic (soil-forming) events which took place during times of lake decline—is one of the most recent developments in the study of the Claron Formation.

Nearly as perplexing as the problem of the origin of the Claron is that of its precise age. Those few fossils that have been recovered are sometimes not well enough preserved to be precisely identified and/or they belong to a species known to range through a great span of geologic time. Moreover, the Claron Formation contains no materials, such as lava flows or volcanic ash, that can be dated by sophisticated techniques based on the decay of radioactive elements.

The position of the Claron beds above the Cretaceous strata at Bryce Canyon made it obvious, even to the earliest geologists, that they were probably of Tertiary age. But, the Tertiary is a long period of time, beginning 66 million years ago and concluding about 1.8 million years ago.

Exactly when in this vast interval was the Claron Formation deposited? No one knows for sure. Tertiary time is subdivided into several epochs, and most geologists agree that the Claron formed in the early part of the Tertiary Period, principally during the Eocene Epoch and perhaps during the preceding Paleocene Epoch. This dates the formation of the Claron at approximately 50 to 60 million years ago. It may be that the upper beds of the Claron Formation are somewhat younger; the lower layers could be a little older.

Recall that the Cretaceous Straight Cliffs and Wahweap formations immediately beneath the Claron are between 80 and 85 million years old. Thus, 20 to 30 million years of time separate the Claron Formation from underlying strata along the angular unconformity. During this unrecorded interval, some important geologic events caused profound changes in the southern Utah landscape. The Western Interior Seaway of the Cretaceous

Period had withdrawn from the Bryce Canyon region by the beginning of the Tertiary, leaving a low plain exposed east of the now subdued highlands, remnants of the old Sevier Orogenic Belt. Then, virtually on the first day of the Tertiary Period, the rumbling early stages of the Laramide Orogeny began to elevate the land. This uplift, related to the activation of faults deep in the Earth's crust, warped and domed the stratified rocks in certain portions of the Colorado Plateau. Several broad anticlines formed as the surface rocks were buckled and lifted. Along the crests of these great arches, the rising land began to capture more and more moisture from ancient storms.

Elevated watersheds gradually evolved from a formerly low and nearly featureless plain. The abundant water flowing off the flanks of the dome-shaped uplifts evidently did not find an outlet to the distant sea. It accumulated in the closed drainage basins of the low surrounding areas, creating numerous small lakes. As the anticlines and domes continued to bulge upward during the early part of the Tertiary Period, these lakes grew larger until they merged into a system of inter-connected lakes.

A few million years later, the lake system extended well into present-day Colorado along the southern border of the Uinta Mountains. Students of this phase of its development call it Green River Lake, after the principal formation which accumulated in it. The lake system, which persisted until the late Eocene Epoch (about 40 million years ago), was comparable in size to the modern Great Lakes of North America.

ANOTHER MISSING CHAPTER: FAULTING, UPLIFT, AND EROSION

By the end of Eocene time, about 37 million years ago, the great lakes of the Tertiary had, for the most part, disappeared. The summits of watersheds elevated during the Laramide Orogeny had been lowered by erosion, reducing their ability to filch moisture from passing storms. The lowlands were choked by thousands of feet of sediment shed from the uplifted areas and rivers began to flow across the basins formerly occupied by the lakes. In addition, the climate appears to have been drier in the middle part of the Tertiary Period than during the earliest stages. It is little wonder, then, that most of the great lakes did not survive beyond the end of the Eocene Epoch.

The Claron Formation at Bryce Canyon National Park varies in thickness from about 300 feet to around 700 feet. In other places, the Claron Formation exceeds 1,000 feet in thickness and includes a sandstone member above the white limestone member. The Claron Formation in the Paunsaugunt region is therefore incomplete. Some of it was removed by erosion prior to the accumulation of the next layer above, the conglomerate at Boat Mesa. The erosion of the uppermost beds of the Claron Formation produced an irregular scoured surface, an unconformity, at the top of the formation. This interval of erosion was probably induced by uplift experienced during the earliest stages of normal faulting in the High Plateaus region. The Fairyland Fault, which passes

The conglomerate at Boat Mesa is exposed at Bryce Point.

beneath Boat Mesa, is one of these early normal faults. It displaces the Claron Formation, but does not affect 35 – 40-million-year-old rocks above the unconformity.

So, it appears that soon after the Claron beds were deposited, faulting began to elevate the old lakebed. Streams cut into the slowly rising land and ultimately removed the upper portion of the Claron Formation, preserving only a partial thickness beneath a cap of later deposits.

THE CONGLOMERATE
AT BOAT MESA:
DEBRIS SHED
FROM RISING LAND

In most places within Bryce Canyon National Park, the Claron Formation is exposed at the surface and forms the caprock along the rim of the Paunsaugunt Plateau. Over broad areas, it is the youngest rock unit in the entire sequence. At Boat Mesa and along the rim from Bryce Point to Inspiration Point, however, the white member of the Claron is overlain by 50 to 100 feet of light brown or gray sandstone and conglomerate. The brownish sandstone is very coarse-grained and commonly contains tan, gray, black, and white pebbles enclosed by the smaller sand grains. The white or light gray layers consist of pebbles and sand bound together with calcite, the same mineral which is found in limestone. Fragments of limestone derived from the Claron Formation below are found in some exposures of the conglomerate.

This sandstone and conglomerate cap on the Claron Formation is not present everywhere in the park, but rather occurs in small, isolated patches. Because these rocks are best represented at Boat Mesa and nearby areas, where they are about 100 feet thick, they have been named the conglomerate at Boat Mesa. Why not the Boat Mesa Conglomerate? Recall that a formation must be a distinctive package of rock layers which have some reasonable lateral or geographic extent. The conglomerate at Boat Mesa is restricted to small patches within Bryce Canyon National Park and has not been identified beyond the park boundaries. Although the deposits of sandstone and conglomerate are similar in a general way to other rock units found in the Tertiary sequences of neighboring regions, a precise equivalence with other formations cannot be demonstrated.

The conglomerate at Boat Mesa is neither extensive nor distinctive enough to be considered a valid geological formation. In such cases, geological convention is to name the strata after the area of best exposure. To help distinguish formations from informal rock units, geologists typically place the geographic portion of the name after the uncapitalized rock name. So, the conglomerate at Boat Mesa is a useful descriptive term; if it were a valid formation, we would call it the Boat Mesa Conglomerate.

Boat Mesa is not the only area where the conglomerate at Boat Mesa can be seen. It is also found around Bryce Point, where visitors stand on good outcrops of it, and along the rim extending north toward Inspiration Point. In the Bryce

Point-Inspiration Point area, the conglomerate rests upon the white member of the Claron Formation. At Boat Mesa, you will see the same material capping the pink member of the Claron.

How can a single sequence of rock layers be deposited at two different horizons? Remember the unconformity. In the Boat Mesa area, erosion completely removed the white member of the Claron. Sand and gravel then accumulated on the rocks of the underlying pink member. At Bryce Point, the erosion was not so deep and the conglomerate was deposited on strata of the white member which had not yet been removed.

Because the conglomerate extends across old structures like the Fairyland Fault without any displacement, we can be certain that such faults were no longer active when the sediment accumulated. Whatever the source of the conglomerate at Boat Mesa, it was probably not associated with uplifts along these old faults. The wavelike uplift which initiated the scouring of the Claron Formation seems to have migrated into other nearby areas during the latter part of the Tertiary Period. The coarse, gravelly sand represented by the conglomerate at Boat Mesa was deposited by vigorous streams flowing from some uplifted highland near the Bryce Canyon region.

The conglomerate at Boat Mesa contains no fossils or other useful indicators of age. We do know that it must be younger than the Claron Formation on which it rests, which is of the Paleocene-Eocene epochs. The interval of erosion following the deposition of the Claron sediments must have been significant, but there is no way of

determining exactly how long it was. The next epoch of the Tertiary Period after the Eocene is the Oligocene (37 – 24 million years ago); the conglomerate at Boat Mesa was probably deposited sometime during this interval. There is some indirect evidence that such dating is reasonable. About 35 million years ago, just after the beginning of the Oligocene Epoch, a violent storm of volcanic activity began in the Sevier Plateau north of the Bryce Canyon region. This volcanic rampage continued for millions of years into the succeeding epochs of the Tertiary Period, constructing massive heaps of smoldering rock erupted from the throats of hundreds of volcanoes. The grains and pebbles in the conglomerate at Boat Mesa consist predominantly of quartz, limestone, and a hard sedimentary rock known as chert. Grains or pebbles derived from volcanic rocks are almost entirely absent from these deposits.

We can infer, then, that the conglomerate at Boat Mesa was deposited before the volcanic conflagration had produced any elevated terrain (such as the Black Mountains which now loom north of the park) to serve as a source of the coarse sediment it contains.

The conglomerate at Boat Mesa was probably derived from uplifts which developed just before the beginning of the volcanic frenzy. Magma, working its way slowly toward the surface along fractures in the underlying rock, could have elevated broad domes prior to the violent explosions. Streams flowing from the rising domes might then have carried sediment from the north into the Bryce Canyon region. As these rivers passed over the lower ground, their channels would have shifted back and forth, leaving a veneer of sand and gravel behind.

Imagine an early Oligocene scene as you stand at the Bryce Point overlook and stare down at the pebbly sandstone. Think of water flowing swift and turbulent in small ribbons braided around sand and gravel bars across a broad plain. Hear the gurgling water and feel the gravel rolling over your toes. Lift your eyes to the north and imagine the plain rising toward the soft silhouettes of mountains on the horizon. Feel the Oligocene breeze on your face as you watch billowy clouds drift along in a satin sky. Then, smelling the damp fragrance of the wet sand at your feet, you hear a low rumble rolling across the landscape. Feel the vibrations when the ground heaves and you stagger for balance on the quivering sand. Watch breathless as one of the distant domes explodes, sending a brilliant glowing cloud swirling from the summit. The shock wave and then the scorching ash and lava close in on you, ravaging the land and annihilating all life.

THE SEVIER RIVER FORMATION: REFUSE OF A VOLCANIC RAMPAGE

The youngest rock unit exposed in the Bryce Canyon area is the Sevier River Formation, which occurs in small patches in the northern extremity of the park. This formation was probably much more extensive in the distant past, but has been removed by erosion everywhere except in the upper Little Henderson Canyon-Cedar Canyon area. Even these outcrops are difficult to spot because the soft, crumbly rocks have weathered into low gray mounds and hummocks which are generally covered by soil and vegetation. Where it is present, the Sevier River Formation rests on the Claron Formation and is generally less than 30 feet thick — a meager remnant of an expansive blanket of rock.

The Sevier River Formation consists of brown or brownish-gray sandstone, interbedded with conglomerate. Even the sandstones are often conglomeratic. The coarse granular rocks are, for the most part, weakly cemented with calcite and quickly disintegrate into soil at the surface. Chunks of rock in the conglomerate may be as large as 8 inches, and many have a relatively sharp, angular form. These features suggest that the sediment in the Sevier River Formation was washed into the Bryce Canyon region by streams flowing from some nearby source. If there had been extensive transport of the sediment from a distant location, we would expect to see much smaller and more rounded fragments.

Perhaps the most revealing aspect of the rocks in the Sevier River Formation is the composition of the grains and fragments within the conglomerate and sandstone. Unlike the conglomerate at Boat Mesa, many of the rock fragments in the Sevier River Formation consist of gray or brownish volcanic materials. The source of the coarse sediment was clearly a nearby volcanic highland. The formation contains fragments of 25-million-year-old volcanic rocks, so it had to have been deposited after those rocks were erupted, eroded, and transported by streams to the Bryce Canyon region. In the Sevier River Valley, where this formation was first defined in the late 1930s, the deposits are thought to be as young as about 2 million years (late Pliocene-early Pleistocene epochs). So, the sediments of the Sevier River Formation seem to have accumulated over the past 20 million years or so (Miocene to Pleistocene epochs), and the formation's precise age no doubt varies from place to place in the High Plateaus region.

During the time that the Sevier River Formation was being deposited, the middle-Tertiary volcanic activity of southwest Utah was reaching its apocalyptic climax. While no volcanoes erupted in the Bryce Canyon region during this time, nearby regions to the north were ablaze. Ash darkened the skies repeatedly and blanketed the surrounding terrain. Seething flows of lava poured from the flanks of the volcanoes and mudslides slithered down their steeper slopes. Streams, some born of the condensation of immense clouds of steam, washed the rubble of devastated peaks into lower regions beyond the volcanoes. The surface of these lowlands became a volcanic junkyard. Today this granular wreckage is called the Sevier River Formation.

Even as the volcanic events of the middle Tertiary Period were underway, stretching forces which elevated the modern High Plateaus began to take effect. Yielding to these new forces, great rifts such as the Sevier and Paunsaugunt faults began to develop sometime in the Miocene Epoch, probably around 16 million years ago. The rate of displacement along these fractures varied through the ensuing eons, but seems to have been greatest between 5 and 8 million years ago, in the late Miocene epoch. The High Plateaus began their incremental rise, gradually emerging as the lofty tablelands which so dazzled Clarence Dutton.

As the Paunsaugunt Plateau rose, agents of erosion began to attack the rock layers formed during earlier intervals of geologic history. Water, wind, and gravity—nature's wrecking crew— worked in concert to efface and obscure. The Sevier River Formation, or at least most of it, was the first victim of intensified erosion in the rising block. Nearly all of this rock unit has been erased from the Bryce Canyon region. Then, the conglomerate at Boat Mesa (where it was present) emerged as the protective cover. Eventually erosion cut even deeper, removing much of the white limestone member of the Claron Formation and penetrating, in places, into the underlying pink member. The erosion which removed much of the younger rock layers created this glorious shrine to the dynamic artistry of geologic processes. Whatever else Bryce Canyon National Park may be, it is certainly a monument to erosion.

EROSION

NATURE SCULPTS A WONDERLAND IN STONE

Erosion is the disintegration of solid rock under the influence of physical, atmospheric, and biological conditions, and the subsequent transport of products of that decay. Erosion is often confused with a similar and simultaneous process known as weathering. Weathering refers to the spontaneous changes in the physical and chemical characteristics of bedrock upon exposure to conditions at the Earth's surface. Weathering can be thought of as the corrosion of rock in place. The dissolution of soluble rock or the reaction of rock components with oxygen in the atmosphere are common examples of chemical weathering, while the opening of fractures within large blocks represents a physical form of weathering. Erosion, on the other hand, describes the broader processes of surface degradation in which weathering is an initial

> > > > > < < < < <

Erosion is relentless, never stops or pauses, and is eternally reshaping the surface of the world around us. Everywhere we look we see rock disintegrating. The freeze-thaw cycles which occur in the Paunsaugunt Plateau region give rise to seasonal ice formations in Mossy Cave (above). Inspiration Point (left).

> > > > > < < < < <

step. Individual rocks weather to produce smaller grains and chemical products, while the cliffs they comprise are eroded when those materials are transported away by water, wind, or gravity.

The weathering and erosion of rock exposures are universal, ever-present characteristics of the Earth's surface. Everywhere we look we see rock disintegrating. We see boulders breaking from sheer cliffs and piling up in great heaps of blocky hunks. We see the inscriptions on headstones in old cemeteries obscured as the rocks decay. We observe mudslides carrying soil down steep slopes, leaving scalloped scars on mountainsides. All these events, and many more, are expressions of the constant fraying of the Earth's surface. Erosion is relentless, never stops or pauses, and is eternally reshaping the surface of the world around us.

Yellow Creek (above) is so named because of the orange and yellow silt it carries away from the eroding cliffs of the Claron Formation in the headwaters region.

The Grottos (right) are large cavities dissolved by water moving through the soluble limestone of the Claron Formation. Water is also capable of eroding rock mechanically through processes such as frost wedging.

In Bryce Canyon National Park, the results of such degradation are both spectacular and unique. Rocks shine with vivid colors produced by weathering of the enclosed minerals. Deep, shadowy channels are cut through the labyrinthine maze of columns, pinnacles, and ridges. The rock pedestals themselves are elaborately sculpted into bizarre forms under the attack of the elements. Vast recesses have been carved into the sheer cliffs. There is nothing, anywhere in the world, to compare to the extraordinary erosional features in Bryce Canyon. Here, erosion has been governed by a combination of factors—the rocks, the terrain, the climate, and time—which has not been duplicated anywhere else on our planet. This wondrous landscape seems unearthly to us because, by virtue of its singularity, it is.

THE AGENTS OF EROSION

The agents of weathering and erosion are as varied as their products. Water, wind, gravity, and living entities are all capable of ravaging bedrock, each in its own unique way. Water, though, can be considered nature's master sculptor. The high surface of the Paunsaugunt Plateau receives an ample amount—about 16 inches annually—of this most effective agent of erosion.

When water falls as rain or snow through the atmosphere, it combines with carbon dioxide to become weakly acidic. Where air is fouled by industrial pollution, the moisture may become highly acidic. When water falls to the ground, its impact alone can dislodge small grains. Acidic

water runs over the rock surface or seeps into cracks and small pores. If the rock contains a mineral which dissolves easily, such as the calcite so abundant in the Claron Formation, the cement holding grains together can be weakened or dissolved completely. The rock begins to crumble. As the water runs off, it can transport loosened grains away. Sometimes raindrops seep into the rock along fractures and freeze. When water freezes, its volume increases, exerting pressure within the crack and causing it to splinter. Through this process, known as frost wedging, the crack becomes larger, more water can enter, more mineral cement is dissolved, more grains are loosened, and more material is available to be washed away.

Gravity also plays an important role in erosion, continually pulling loose rock and soil toward lower elevations. The gravitational movement of materials may be either slow or rapid. Soil particles may gradually slide or roll downhill in a gravity-driven process called creep. On the other hand, blocks of rock may move suddenly in the form of rockfalls and landslides. The steep slopes and vertical cliffs in the Bryce Canyon area are particularly conducive to the effectiveness of gravity as an agent of erosion.

Living organisms may also contribute to the process of erosion. The roots of shrubs and trees, penetrating along minute cracks in bedrock, may exert enough force to widen and deepen the fractures. Some plants also produce acidic compounds as a by-product of their life processes or as a product of their decay. These acids may

In the vicinity of Paria View (right), numerous pockets and cavities in the cliffs are the result of dissolution of limestone in the Claron Formation.

attack the soil and rocks, accelerating weathering on the surface.

Wind can sometimes be an effective agent of erosion, but it is not nearly as important here as water or gravity. Only the smallest fragments of rock and soil can be moved by the wind and nothing at all can be transported when the air is calm. Furthermore, plant cover, such as the lush forest thriving atop the Paunsaugunt Plateau tends to protect loose rock and soil particles from wind erosion.

Every exposure of rock is subjected to the simultaneous attack of all these agents of erosion. Water, gravity, organisms, and wind all work together, each enhancing the ability of the others to modify the landscape. Frost wedging may, for example, develop cracks within the rocks of a cliff face, while running water removes material from its base. The unsupported block may then tumble away under the influence of gravity (this is known as slab failure). How the bedrock yields to this combined assault depends on factors such as rock composition and internal structure, climate, and configuration of the terrain.

ROCKS, CLIMATE, AND CLIFFS: OVERSEERS OF EROSION

In the strata of the Claron Formation the tangled badlands, pastel pinnacles called hoodoos, and dusky slotlike defiles have developed under the onslaught of the elements. Recall that the Claron is divided into a lower pink limestone member and an upper white limestone member. Due to differences

in their makeup, the two members erode in different ways. Nevertheless, overall similarities are important in influencing the erosion of both. Calcite, which makes up the bulk of each member, is a highly soluble mineral.

Dissolution of the rocks in the Claron Formation is most apparent in the white limestone member, which contains fewer impurities than the limestone in the pink member. Deep cavities called the Grottos west of Bryce Point have formed as water, seeping through the pure limestones of the white member, dissolved the calcite. The openings in the narrow limestone ridge extending north from the Grottos, known as the Wall of Windows, probably originated as similar solution pockets. Further erosion has deepened the cavities and cut a gully which separates the "wall" from the cliffs of the rim to the west.

The many hues of the Claron Formation, particularly in the pink member, add an elegant dimension to the magnificent landforms produced by erosion. As we suggested in our earlier discussion of the Claron, this unique palette is largely the result of oxidation, a form of chemical weathering which occurs when oxygen in water or air combines with metallic elements in the rock. The rocks of the Claron Formation contain small amounts of several metals, among which iron and manganese are the two most important to the production of bright colors through oxidation. Iron and manganese tend to be more common in the pink member (which, of course, is why it's red in weathered exposures), while the purer white limestone member contains fewer of these metallic

66

The fluted sides of the hoodoos seen from Sunset Point (right) result from the variation in resistance to weathering in the layered rocks of the Claron Formation. Gray dolomite layers are more durable than limestone or siltstone and project from the hoodoos and walls as ledges.

impurities and is not so strongly banded with color.

Even where the metals are present, they are not always oxidized to the same degree in adjacent layers. Water and air can move through some porous rocks, such as sandstone or sandy limestone, easily while mudstone and shale are almost impenetrable. The varying concentration of metals in the rocks, coupled with the differences in the degree of oxidation in individual layers, is responsible for the multiple bands of colors seen in the cliff faces and the hoodoos of the park. Pale red zones, bright purple horizons, luminous pink layers, and rusty yellow partitions all reflect these variations.

The irregular shapes and forms of sculpted pinnacles and pillars developed from the Claron Formation are as striking as their bright colors. Successive and uneven hollows and projecting ledges alternate up the bizarre columns. This unevenness results because the various layers from which the hoodoos erode do not weather at the same rate. The limestones, for instance, tend to erode more slowly than the sandy strata. Recall, also, that some of the limestone layers contain dolomite, a magnesium-rich carbonate mineral. The dolomitic limestone intervals are more resistant to weathering than the non-dolomitic layers and often project outward as a ledge on the fluted surface of a column.

An additional attribute of the rocks in Bryce Canyon has a strong influence on the striking style of erosion unique to this area. Stresses related to the uplift of the Paunsaugunt Plateau and to the earlier thrusting, have generated a network of fractures within the rocks comprised of small-scale faults and joints. Joints differ from faults in that there is no relative movement of blocks on either side—joints are simply cracks in the bedrock. The small-scale faults, on the other hand, show evidence of movement in the form of striations (scratches) which reveal the direction of relative movement.

The rocks of Bryce Canyon, and particularly the Claron Formation, are splintered by two main sets of intersecting fractures. One set consists of numerous parallel fractures which trend in a northwest direction, while the other set of cracks runs to the northeast. These two crisscross each other, dividing the Claron Formation into a splintered mass of blocks bounded by the intersecting fractures. Such a fracture pattern expedites overall erosion by creating more opportunities for interactions between rock and water. The joints also serve as a zone of weakness along which entire slabs of rock can plunge from cliff faces. Furthermore, the fractures serve to accelerate erosion as water trickles down through the cleft, dissolving limestone and washing away the less-soluble silt, clay, and sand. Many of the narrow defiles which separate the hoodoos and ornate walls of stone in Bryce Canyon represent joints or small faults greatly enlarged by erosion.

The climate of Bryce Canyon also exerts an important influence on the process of erosion. Encouraging abundant rainfall, the high altitude of the plateau is also responsible for relatively cool temperatures. The mean annual temperature at the visitor center in the park is about 5°C (40°F), and

an average of 200 days each year, on south-facing slopes, the temperature fluctuates above and below freezing. This high frequency of freeze-thaw cycles accelerates the frost-wedging process, leading to rapid disintegration of the fractured bedrock. Much of the moisture on the Paunsaugunt Plateau comes in the form of brief, but intense, summer thunderstorms. During August, the wettest month in the park, torrential rains often fall so fast that little can be absorbed by the soil or seep into the rock. During such squalls, much of the rain cascades over the rim in small, silt-laden rivulets. This muddy runoff, carrying a great amount of abrasive sediment, scours the small channels and gullies like a strip of sandpaper, leaving deep, bare furrows behind. These countless gullies converging toward the bottoms of the canyons produce the great embayments known as amphitheaters along the rim. Eventually, the small streams gather into larger creeks which, in turn, flow out into the Paria River system and, slowly but surely, to the Pacific Ocean.

In addition to the rocks and the climate, terrain in the Bryce Canyon region plays a significant role in orchestrating the patterns of erosion. The eastern escarpment of the Paunsaugunt Plateau is characterized by steep and rugged topography. Water draining to the east flows swiftly down very steep slopes. The plunging gullies and surfaces below the rim are vigorously eroded by energetic streams of water. If the same rocks were exposed in more gently inclined terrain, we would see fewer stream-eroded features. Steep terrain also increases the potential for gravity-induced failure

of rocks in the cliffs. Landslides, mudflows, and rockfalls occur with unusually high frequency in the park, particularly after a summer deluge has saturated the loose soil. If you walk along any of the trails in the park after a good summer thunderstorm, you will note small piles and mounds of pebbles and mud spread out across the trail. Occasionally, the landslides are very large and there are several places in the lower terrain beneath the rim where ancient landslide or mudflow masses can be observed. The Hat Shop, with its unique crowned pillars, is an especially picturesque exposure of an ancient landslide mass. Rockfalls are rarely witnessed in the park, but over the canyon's long history, they have played an important role in the erosion of the rim. Large blocks of limestone resting on the soft gray hills below the cliffs testify to many rockfalls in the past. The sheer cliffs and jointed nature of the limestone in the Claron Formation combine to increase the frequency of this dramatic gravity-driven form of erosion.

Little by little, under the destructive influence of all these factors, the eastern escarpment of the Paunsaugunt Plateau is crumbling. The cliff face continues to recede to the west. As the rim of the plateau retreats through erosion by water and gravity-driven events, the root systems of some of the trees near the cliffs are exposed. Very good examples can be seen at Sunrise Point and Paria View. The age of a tree can be established through examination of its annual growth rings. Comparing the age of these trees against the amount of material removed to expose their roots, we can

Diagonal fractures sweeping across the hoodoos in Fairyland Canyon (left) mark the position of small thrust faults.

The unique turreted hoodoos in the Hat Shop (above) were eroded from the deposits of an ancient landslide.

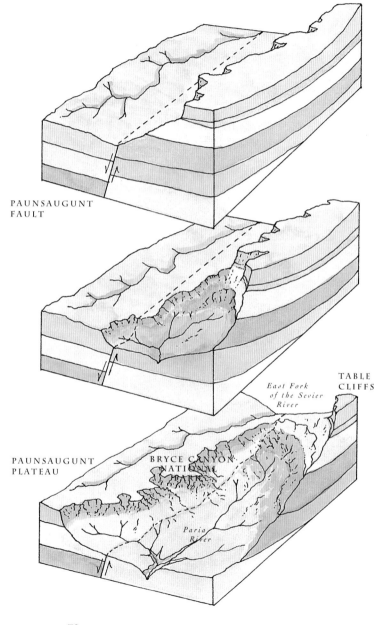

PAUNSAUGUNT
FAULT

East Fork
of the Sevier
River

TABLE
CLIFFS

PAUNSAUGUNT
PLATEAU

BRYCE CANYON
NATIONAL
PARK

Paria
River

estimate the rate at which the cliff is receding. Where this has been done, the rate of cliff retreat is between one and four feet per century.

As the cliffs recede, amphitheaters cut into the rim of the Paunsaugunt Plateau become larger. Each of these scalloped embayments is carved by the Paria River or one of its tributaries—Campbell Creek, Bryce Creek, Yellow Creek, Willis Creek, and many others. The Paria River itself has carved a basin, the Tropic (or Paria) Amphitheater, which is so large that it is difficult to see in its entirety. In the bottom of the amphitheaters you will notice that the main channel of each creek branches into many smaller gullies fanning out toward the base of the cliffs and walls curving around the upper end of each hollow basin. As erosion continues, the small gullies become longer and deeper, and the amphitheater is enlarged. This lengthening of channels and gullies by erosion of rock near the head of a stream is called headward erosion.

The expanse of low land seen to the east from the rim of the park represents just a portion of the vast bowl of erosion created by the Paria and its tributaries. The crumbling rim of the plateau at Bryce Canyon constitutes the western edge of this enormous erosional basin. Like the smaller creeks which flow into it, the southeast-flowing Paria has extended its channel through the process of headward erosion. The amphitheater developed at the river's upper end has continually expanded to the northwest over the past few million years. As the Tropic Amphitheater developed, the southern rim of Bryce Canyon National Park was first affected by headward erosion of Paria River tributaries. The escarpment in the northern portion of the park was affected later, when the expanding Tropic Amphitheater reached it. Varying degrees of erosion, coupled with the differences in elevation along the northeast-sloping rim, have bestowed on each segment of the eroded plateau fringe unique landforms and distinctive characteristics.

The southern portion of the escarpment, in the area around Rainbow Point, is characterized by two levels of sheer cliffs which hang high above spacious amphitheaters carved by such Paria tributaries as Willis Creek, Sheep Creek, and Heward Creek. The undulating floors of the basins lie 1,500 – 2,000 feet below vertical cliffs.

The entire thickness of the Claron Formation has been penetrated by downcutting streams and the softer Cretaceous strata are exposed over broad areas. The uppermost cliff was formed by slab failure, the splitting off of large blocks of limestone caprock (from the white member of the Claron Formation) along joints. This process is also important in the formation of the lower cliff from a thick layer of jointed limestone in the red member of the Claron Formation. Large blocks of fallen limestone can be seen lying on the smooth slopes at the base of the lower cliff in a number of places beneath the southern rim. Between the two vertical cliffs, an interval of softer reddish-brown beds has eroded into steep slopes supporting short pillars and columns. The southern portion of the escarpment is the most deeply eroded segment of the rim and has retreated farther to the west than have the northern sections.

Between Boat Mesa and Bryce Point, in the central part of the park, the amphitheaters are smaller and shallower, generally descending less than 1,000 feet below the popular viewpoints. As erosion continues in this middle portion of the escarpment, the amphitheaters will become wider and deeper while the rim steadily retreats to the west.

This part of the park will eventually look much like the southern segment. But for now its cliffs are less precipitous, and downcutting by streams such as Bryce Creek, Campbell Creek, and their many tributaries is the main erosional process. Because the cliffs in this sector are less imposing, slab failure is of secondary importance in the erosion of the rim.

The edge of the plateau swings east here because there has not been enough time for eroding streams to undercut the caprock and force the cliffs into full western retreat. The Claron Formation extends from the edge of the escarpment, where either the red member or the white member may form the caprock, to very near the bottoms of the amphitheaters.

Cretaceous exposures are limited to the lowest areas adjacent to the incised gullies. The most conspicuous erosional features of this middle segment are the ornate hoodoos for which the park is famous. The development of these pinnacles will be discussed in the next section.

The area north of Boat Mesa—from Fairyland Canyon to Tropic Canyon—constitutes the northern segment of the escarpment. Here, headward erosion of streams descending into the

Headward erosion by the Paria River and its tributaries (left) has carved the Tropic Amphitheater. The unique landforms of Bryce Canyon National Park have developed over the past 15 million years on the western wall of the amphitheater.

Because the Tropic Amphitheater developed from the south, the northern portion of Bryce Canyon National Park has experienced less erosion. The park can be divided into three sections based on the depth and degree of erosion. The northern segment (top) has landforms characteristic of moderate erosion, while the southern section (bottom) is the most heavily eroded. The differences in the degree of erosion of the Bryce escarpment reflect the varying length of the erosional histories: brief in the north and long in the south.

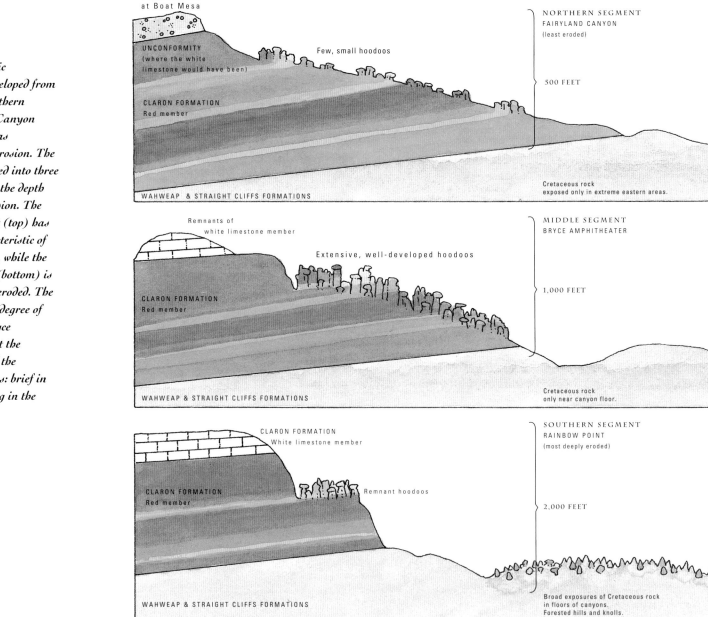

Conglomerate at Boat Mesa

UNCONFORMITY (where the white limestone would have been)

CLARON FORMATION
Red member

Few, small hoodoos

WAHWEAP & STRAIGHT CLIFFS FORMATIONS

NORTHERN SEGMENT
FAIRYLAND CANYON
(least eroded)

500 FEET

Cretaceous rock exposed only in extreme eastern areas.

Remnants of white limestone member

Extensive, well-developed hoodoos

CLARON FORMATION
Red member

WAHWEAP & STRAIGHT CLIFFS FORMATIONS

MIDDLE SEGMENT
BRYCE AMPHITHEATER

1,000 FEET

Cretaceous rock only near canyon floor.

CLARON FORMATION
White limestone member

CLARON FORMATION
Red member

Remnant hoodoos

WAHWEAP & STRAIGHT CLIFFS FORMATIONS

SOUTHERN SEGMENT
RAINBOW POINT
(most deeply eroded)

2,000 FEET

Broad exposures of Cretaceous rock in floors of canyons. Forested hills and knolls.

upper end of the Tropic Amphitheater has only recently begun to alter the landscape. Consequently, the difference in elevation between the plateau surface and the canyon bottoms is only about 500 feet.

Downcutting streams in this northern portion of the park have yet to dissect completely the Claron Formation, which is exposed from the rim of the plateau to the bottom of the gullies. The only exposures of Cretaceous rocks here are beyond the Paunsaugunt Fault, where the upward movement of the eastern block has brought these older strata to the surface.

The terrain, low ridges separated by moderate ravines, seems subdued compared to the vertical cliffs and deeply furrowed badlands of the south. There are not as many resistant layers in the northern segment of the Claron Formation and the hoodoos, which are so splendidly developed in the middle segment, are fewer and less impressive.

The roughly 18-mile-long escarpment in Bryce Canyon National Park offers an opportunity to view the effects of varying amounts of erosion simply by examining landforms in its different segments. Most visitors to the park focus their attention on the popular viewpoints and trails in the middle segment between Bryce Point and Sunrise Point.

Though the northern and southern segments may seem less spectacular, both are worthy of exploration. They provide superb opportunities to learn about the dynamics of erosion and the influence of rock types, terrain, and time on that fundamental geological process.

HOODOOS: GRAND ICONS OF EROSION

Of all the magnificent products of erosion in Bryce Canyon National Park, it is the baroque pillars called hoodoos which are most symbolic of this enchanting landscape. They also spark the imaginations and curiosity of visitors to the park, many of whom wonder about their origin. The formation of hoodoos is a complex multistage process governed by a variety of factors. Hoodoos are not the end result of any sequence of events, but are more accurately thought of as temporary consequences in the ongoing process of erosion. Hoodoos are ephemeral—new columns form while older columns are destroyed—and erosion is both their creator and, eventually, their executioner.

The development of hoodoos begins at the rim of the plateau in the Claron Formation, as headward erosion cuts through the bedrock exposed along the escarpment. Recall that this rock unit consists of interlayered limestone, sandstone, and mudstone. As we have seen, each of these basic rock types varies considerably in composition and texture. The unique response of each layer to the processes of natural decay is embraced by the term differential erosion, which means simply that individual rock types are affected by erosion in different ways and at different rates. The bizarre form of the hoodoos is largely a reflection of the differential erosion of the Claron Formation.

Gullies are usually developed in the caprock of the rim along joints, where the fractures accelerate downcutting. As headward erosion of the

Thor's Hammer is one of the best-known formations in Bryce Canyon National Park.

THE ORIGIN OF HOODOOS

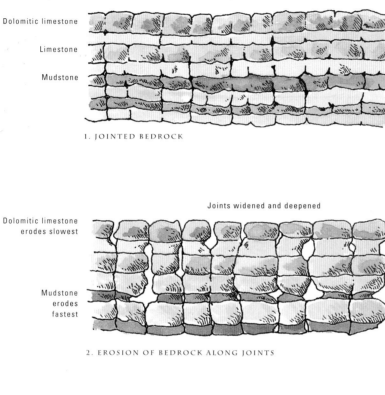

Dolomitic limestone

Limestone

Mudstone

1. JOINTED BEDROCK

Joints widened and deepened

Dolomitic limestone
erodes slowest

Mudstone
erodes
fastest

2. EROSION OF BEDROCK ALONG JOINTS

3. COLUMNS SEPARATED ALONG JOINTS,
THEN CARVED BY DIFFERENTIAL EROSION

"Hats" of
resistant
rock

escarpment continues, the gullies along the rim become deeper and wider. Between the deepening furrows, walls of rock begin to emerge where downcutting is less active. The rock walls are eroding of course, but at a far slower rate than are the gullies, where water is continually scouring the bedrock. Eventually, a layer of resistant rock, such as dolomitic limestone, is exposed at the top of the walls. This new caprock partially protects the softer material beneath it from rapid erosion.

The sides of the rock walls, however, become vertical as runoff along the slope scours the softer material at their base. Remember that the amphitheaters are continually expanding, their curving margins penetrating farther into the edge of the plateau. Slopes at any point within the amphitheater recede into the bedrock of the escarpment as the perimeter of the amphitheater grows larger. Walls of rock between gullies are less affected by this recession of the slopes because they are more protected by the caprock. Ultimately, the walls become elongated and rise higher and higher above the receding slopes at their base. Some of these walls eventually come to resemble great curtains of stone extending from the rim down into the depths of the amphitheaters. Where the walls have become relatively thin, they are known as fins, and may rise hundreds of feet above neighboring defiles. Walls this high often have more than one layer of resistant rock, but there is always a prominent ledge of durable material at the top, protecting the underlying strata.

Once the fins of stone form, the slopes at their

Hoodoos develop through the erosion of jointed bedrock of varying resistance to the elements (far left).

Hoodoos emerging from a fin in Fairyland Canyon (left).

base continue to erode, as do the sides and tops of the walls of rock along joint planes and other zones of weakness. Often, the sides of the fins become coated with a natural "stucco" consisting of the granular debris of weathering, cemented in place by calcium carbonate derived from the dissolution of limestone, and deposited on the vertical face by water dripping from higher ledges and caps. This protective coating, which is sometimes called dripstone, can impede the decay of the fins while the joints are deepened and widened from above. The result is that crude, irregular columns gradually emerge from a once-continuous drape of rock. The hoodoos rise higher and higher along the ragged fringe of the fin as more material is removed by erosion along the fractures. Simultaneously, the slope retreats back into the head of the amphitheater.

Inevitably, even the pillars, protected to some degree by dripstone and caprock, succumb to the relentless attack of the elements, and the hoodoos begin to crumble. Large blocks of resistant caprock, the remains of vanished hoodoos, can be seen strewn across smooth slopes in the lower portions of many amphitheaters in the park. As the amphitheaters continue to expand, cutting into the edge of the plateau, their floors are deepened until they intersect the soft gray Cretaceous strata beneath the Claron Formation. Eventually, continued erosion of these relatively weak strata will create a broad rolling basin, its sinuous hills and hummocks separating shallow creeks which run downstream toward their convergence. Meanwhile, in the high amphitheater walls,

newborn pillars will emerge to replace those which perish in the endless war between rock and weather.

For as long as the Paunsaugunt Plateau exists, we will have hoodoo kingdoms along the transitory edge of the tablelands. But, even the plateau itself is doomed. Unless some future geologic disturbance intervenes, the end result of the vigorous erosion witnessed along this escarpment will be a complete leveling of the land surface. Gone will be the lush forests, the spectacular badlands, and the sweeping vistas of the Grand Staircase. Thankfully, these changes in the landscape will be as slow as they are certain. Though the escarpment is constantly changing, we will have the scenic splendor of Bryce Canyon to enjoy for several million years to come.

Fluted columns along the Queen's Garden Trail (left) show the artistry of erosion.

Natural "stucco" consists of the granular debris of weathering cemented in place by calcium carbonate deposited on the vertical face of rock by water dripping from higher ledges (above).

EPILOGUE
THE TREASURE OF BRYCE CANYON NATIONAL PARK

What do people gain from visiting Bryce Canyon National Park? The answer to that question is probably as diverse as the millions of visitors entering the park. You will find your own unique magic in the gorgeous vistas, the imposing cliffs, the halcyon forests, the timid wildlife, or the bountiful meadows. Even the most passive observer in this natural panorama discovers a soothing tranquility. The aesthetic appeal of the park is undeniable and profoundly rewarding.

Yet, there is something else to be gained from your visit, a prize which may be even more valuable than fond memories of a beautiful land. That priceless treasure is knowledge and understanding of the intricate weave of rock, time, and life which has fashioned this exquisite land and placed us here before it. Every corner of the park is a window into the intimate

> > > > > < < < < <
Only by knowing the land from the geological perspective can we truly understand it, love it, and care for it. The land has its own magic. Every rock face affords opportunities to explore times and events far removed from our own day-to-day experiences. Winter moonrise at Sunset Point (above). Inspiration Point in winter (left).
> > > > > < < < < <

workings of our planet, and every rock face affords opportunities to explore times and events far removed from our own day-to-day experiences.

To grasp these lessons, we must extend our minds beyond their routine limits of space and time and struggle to envision things we can never directly experience. This quest for understanding of the Earth and its history embodies the quintessential spirit of geology. And, in this effort, it is not the facts and figures about Bryce Canyon that matter as much as the struggle to comprehend their meaning and significance.

Just what is the value of understanding the geologic history of the land? Above all, it is the deepening of our intimacy with the planet from which we arose and of which we are a significant part. That understanding breeds a special kind of love for the land.

Love spawns respect, and respect begets care. Though we often view ourselves as detached from the natural world, we are bound here as much as the mule deer in the forest, the pine trees clinging to the cliffs, and the rain falling from the clouds. We are compelled to know our own history as a species and to understand our place in the flow of time and matter. Only by knowing the land from the geological perspective can we truly understand it, love it, and care for it. The fanning of that inner passion for knowledge, and the fostering of a spiritual commitment to use it wisely, is the greatest benefit derived from our ageless quest.

As you gaze across these magnificent vistas, try to see the stories engraved in the landscape and feel the overwhelming history which surrounds you. Surrender to the tales of former worlds spoken softly by the stone monarchs. Return, again and again, to be nurtured and revitalized by the beauty and the wonder of Bryce Canyon National Park.

Sunrise, at Bryce Point (left) and Farview Point (above).

The Geology of Bryce Canyon's
UNIQUE LANDSCAPES

RAINBOW POINT

At the south end of the park are the twin viewpoints of Yovimpa Point, with its southern vista, and Rainbow Point facing north. From Rainbow Point, the view along the escarpment reveals some unique aspects of the rocks and distinctive patterns of erosion in this area.

Rainbow Point is perched atop a thick cap of creamy tan limestone belonging to the upper white member of the Claron Formation. As you trace this cap along the escarpment to the north, notice how uneven it is. The layers are thick and massive in spots, thin in others, and totally absent in a few. The changing depth of the caprock reflects both a variance in the original thickness of these layers and the differing rates of modern erosion from place to place along the rim.

Beneath the white cap are red-colored layers of the pink

> > > > > < < < < <
Rainbow Point is perched atop a thick cap of creamy tan limestone belonging to the upper white member of the Claron Formation. Beneath the white cap are red-colored layers of the pink limestone member of the Claron. The deep red-brown color is developed through the oxidation of small amounts of iron in the sandstone (left, above).

> > > > > < < < < <

limestone member of the Claron. Note the deep red-brown color of the slope-forming rocks immediately beneath the caprock. This color is developed through the oxidation of small amounts of iron in the sandstone and mudstone. The "pink limestone member" is so named because limestone is the dominant rock, but granular rocks such as sandstone and mudstone are also present and are unusually well represented here at the southern extremity of the park. The sandstone and mudstone in this interval are weakly cemented with calcite; they weather rapidly to form the steep, smooth slope below the upper cliff. Below the red slope, a second high cliff, decorated with numerous hoodoos, emerges from a thick sequence of limestone. Lower still, exposed across the broad and hilly floor of the Willis Creek Basin, are outcrops of the Straight Cliffs and

Wahweap formations of Cretaceous age. The low gray ridges, punctuated occasionally by ledges of relatively resistant sandstone are an expression of the ease with which this soft material yields to the agents of erosion.

The southern end of the escarpment is the most deeply eroded portion of the rim. Note how extensive are the exposures of Cretaceous strata in the low basin before you. This entire amphitheater was once protected by a continuous sheet of limestone and other rock in the Claron Formation. All of that overlying material, and much of the older gray rock beneath it, has been removed by erosion of the eastern edge of the Paunsaugunt Plateau. Notice the eastern swing of the escarpment as you follow it north. This southernmost segment of the rim has receded farther to the west than has any other portion. The unique physiographic character of the rim at Rainbow Point is the result of its relatively long erosional history. To the north — farther upstream of the ancient river channel — headward erosion in the Paria River system only recently began to take effect.

Carefully examine the gray exposures of Cretaceous rocks in the sprawling amphitheater below Rainbow Point. The layering in these rocks is difficult to see because the outcrops are partly covered with brush, but you may be able to discern faint bedding in some areas. Notice that the strata on the west side of the basin, just below the pink and white cliffs, are sloping very gently to the west. Now, looking north-northeast, try to find a location near the lower end of the amphitheater where you can identify layering in these same rocks. Which way are the layers tilted? You may notice that there has been a reversal in the direction of tilting; that the strata on the east side of the basin are dipping gently to the east. If you can see this subtle feature in the obscure outcrops below you, you have found the Bryce Canyon Anticline!

Ponderosa Ridge, the prominent ledge of red and pink rock projecting to the northeast from below Rainbow Point, points the way to another interesting geological feature. Follow the ridge until it seems to end at a small, smooth summit. (Actually, it bends to the east and descends toward lower ground, but this part of the ridge is not visible from Rainbow Point.) From this summit, extend your view to the long ridge across the main channel of lower Willis Creek. Study the distant rock exposures along this east-west ridge on either side of the small summit in the foreground which partially obscures your view. To the east (right, as you face north) of the summit, at the top of an extensive bench, notice the exposure of gray rocks — shading down from darker to lighter — with thin red bands at the base. To the west (left) of the summit, the outcrops are of poorly bedded, gray-brown strata which seem much different from those on the opposite side.

The small summit on Ponderosa Ridge, which we have used for reference, points directly at the Paunsaugunt Fault in the distant background. The red-banded, light gray strata to the east belong to the Jurassic-age Entrada Formation (about 170 million years old). The darker gray-brown layer

above the Entrada Formation is the Dakota Formation. To the west of the fault, on its down-dropped side, the younger Straight Cliffs and Wahweap formations are exposed. So, although the Paunsaugunt Fault itself is difficult to see from Rainbow Point, its effects are visible all around. In the distant background, across the low basin carved by the Paria River, the Table Cliffs Plateau looms against the northeastern horizon. The walls of this plateau expose the red and white strata of the Claron Formation, equivalent to those at Rainbow Point, but over 1,000 feet higher due to displacement on the Paunsaugunt Fault.

Gray and tan Cretaceous rock layers are exposed in the lower slopes seen in the far distance from Rainbow Point.

89

YOVIMPA POINT

Although Yovimpa Point is just a short distance from Rainbow Point, it provides a very different geological perspective because it faces south, overlooking the Grand Staircase. The vista from Yovimpa Point is the most expansive of any in the park, sweeping from the plateau skyline on the western horizon to the remote mountains of the Four Corners region fading into the eastern panorama.

Yovimpa Point is perched upon outcrops of the Claron Formation along the southern edge of the Paunsaugunt Plateau. The cliffs below are the Pink Cliffs, highest step on the Grand Staircase. Immediately below the rim at Yovimpa Point are the typically smooth and gullied outcrops of the Straight Cliffs and Wahweap formations, partly obscured by juniper and pinyon trees, in Corral Hollow and Mutton Hollow.

> > > > > < < < < <

The vista from Yovimpa Point sweeps from the plateau skyline on the western horizon to the Four Corners region to the east. The southern margin of the Paunsaugunt Plateau is seen from Yovimpa Point (above). No Man's Mesa is surrounded by the White Cliffs beyond the Claron Formation exposures at Yovimpa Point (left).

> > > > > < < < < <

These hills and slopes are the Gray Cliffs, a relatively indistinct element of the Grand Staircase. Farther south, the land rises gently toward the next series in the descending stairway. The White Cliffs, exposures of the 180-million-year-old Navajo Sandstone, are partly visible at the end of the rise. No Man's Mesa is a small plateau separated from the main line of cliffs by deep canyons and completely encircled by the White Cliffs. Mollie's Nipple, the sharp peak projecting near the crest of the White Cliffs, is composed of Navajo Sandstone, despite its volcanic appearance. In the distant background, the rise of the Vermillion Cliffs can be seen when the air is clear, as it usually is in the High Plateaus. The only element of the Grand Staircase which cannot be seen from Yovimpa Point is the Chocolate Cliffs, a rather low promontory

Far to the south the surface of the Kaibab Plateau arches across the distant horizon (far left).

Far to the east the silhouette of Navajo Mountain looms above the horizon like a misty purple bulge (left).

which is concealed behind and beneath the higher terrain in the foreground. Far to the south, the surface of the Kaibab Plateau arches across the distant horizon. Through the elevated dome of this great uplift, the Colorado River carved the Grand Canyon.

Far to the east, the silhouette of Navajo Mountain looms above the horizon like a misty purple bulge. Navajo Mountain is one of several isolated igneous peaks in the Colorado Plateau. Other igneous mountains include the LaSal Mountains, the Henry Mountains (visible from other viewpoints in the park), the Abajo Mountains, and several peaks in Colorado and New Mexico. Though the rocks of Navajo Mountain are almost entirely sedimentary, they have been distended upward by the ascent of magma into the core of the peak. This magma is approximately the same age as the igneous rocks in the Sevier Plateau north of Bryce Canyon, and was probably derived from a similar source.

NATURAL BRIDGE OVERLOOK
AGUA CANYON, FARVIEW & PONDEROSA POINTS

The Natural Bridge Overlook is dominated by an impressive span of rock arching more than 125 feet above a steep gully descending from the rim. The arch represents another unique feature produced by the diverse patterns of erosion in Bryce Canyon.

Natural bridges are formed when running water carves out a slot or opening beneath a span of preserved rock. Typically, they form on the outer bank of a sharp bend in a streambed where rushing water most actively scours the rock. By this definition, the Natural Bridge in Bryce is really not a bridge at all. Technically, it is more similar to an arch, which forms through the combined effects of several erosional processes.

Natural Bridge probably originated as a fin of limestone dividing two small, steep gullies. Water running down a gully

> > > > > < < < < <

Natural bridges are formed when running water carves out a slot or opening beneath a span of preserved, harder rock. Natural Bridge is a wall of limestone perforated by the combined attack of water, ice, frost wedging, and gravity (above). From Farview Point you can see down into the basin of Heward Creek (left).

> > > > > < < < < <

alongside the fin carved a hollow recess into the base of the wall of pink limestone. Eventually, the pocket became deep enough to penetrate the width of the fin, and a small opening developed near its base. Meanwhile, frost wedging and gravity attacked the slopes leading down from the rim. The escarpment gradually receded, isolating the perforated fin. Continued erosion enlarged the opening in the fin: the gully beneath it was scoured by running water, blocks of rock above it were loosened through frost wedging, and collapsing fragments were pulled from the fin and the widening arch by gravity.

This arch, like most other erosional landforms in the park, is doomed. The narrow neck of rock supporting its southern end will someday succumb to continued erosion. One day, after the bridge crashes to the steep slope below

The head of Agua Canyon at sunset (far left). The prominent hoodoos are capped by resistant white limestone of the Claron Formation.

Colorful exposures of the Claron Formation can be seen from the head of Ponderosa Canyon (left).

and the blocks vanish down the incline, only two pillars of rock will stand to mark its position. Then, as the escarpment recedes farther and farther to the west. even those pillars will disappear under the relentless attack of the elements. There is no way to know when the arch will collapse, but we can be certain that it is edging ever closer to ruin, even as we examine it today.

In the area around the Natural Bridge viewpoint, at places such as Farview Point, Agua Canyon, and Ponderosa Point, the Claron Formation exhibits other aspects of its changeable character. At each of these viewpoints, the varying colors, diverse patterns of erosion, and differences in rock texture combine to present a unique panorama along the east facing escarpment.

PARIA VIEW

The sweeping vista below Paria View includes several interesting geological features. From the parking area, the trail leads southwest across the white limestone member of the Claron Formation. Notice that these rocks have eroded to form sheer cliffs resting on the pink limestone member, which has weathered into a maze of hoodoos about 150 feet below the rim. Walking down the short trail to the viewpoint, you will notice the exposed roots of many trees dangling precariously at the top of the fearsome cliffs. As the cliffs recede, their caprock is undermined by removal of the softer rock below it, and loose soil along the top of the rim is washed down the gullies, leaving the tree roots exposed. Trees along the cliff edge here are doomed. They will someday follow the rimrocks into the depths of the abyss before you. Along the rim to the north are the

> > > > > < < < < <

Three of the five layers in the Grand Staircase are visible from here: the Pink Cliffs you stand on, the subdued Gray Cliffs in the floor of the canyon, and the distant White Cliffs. The green meadow on the floor of the canyon (left) marks Yellow Spring where water flows from the fractured rock along the Peekaboo Fault. Paria View (above).

> > > > > < < < < <

decaying remains of trees which have already started that journey. Typical rates of cliff retreat at Bryce Canyon National Park are between 1 and 4 feet per century.

A bowl-shaped amphitheater carved by the headwaters of Yellow Creek sprawls below the viewpoint. At the bottom of this basin, the soft gray hills and ridges are underlain by the Straight Cliffs Formation. Trace Yellow Creek downstream until it makes a sharp bend to the east around a prominent cliff of yellowish-gray sandstone. This is one of the thicker sandstone intervals in the Straight Cliffs Formation. Just above the cliff is a reddish patch of alluvium consisting of sand, silt and pebbles eroded from the Claron Formation. This material was deposited by the ancient ancestor of Yellow Creek before the stream had cut down to its present level. Follow the slope up

Lush vegetation grows around Yellow Spring where the Peekaboo Fault crosses the Yellow Creek Canyon (right).

Close-up of the Cretaceous rocks exposed along lower Yellow Creek (far right).

from the red patch of alluvium to a brown cap of sandstone on an east-trending ridge. This small turret of sandstone is in the lower part of the Wahweap Formation, which is very thin in this area due to erosion across the axis of the Bryce Canyon Anticline. Note that the red rocks of the Claron Formation begin just above the level of the Wahweap outcrop.

The small verdant patch on the floor of the amphitheater marks the location of Yellow Spring. Water issuing from this spring rises to the surface through fractured rock along the Peekaboo Fault. It is difficult to see any displacement of the rock layers around the spring because the vista from Paria View is to the east across the fault, not along its north-south trend.

In the distance, rolling gray hills eroded from the Tropic and Dakota formations extend outward to a broad surface, sloping gently to the north. This surface of erosion is developed across relatively soft rocks of Jurassic age (180 million years old). Beyond, light-colored Navajo Sandstone is exposed at the top of the dissected White Cliffs. Three of the five components in the Grand Staircase are visible here: the Pink Cliffs you stand on, the subdued Gray Cliffs in the floor of the canyon before you, and the distant White Cliffs.

BRYCE POINT
AND THE PEEKABOO LOOP TRAIL

Bryce Point is one of the most scenic overlooks in the park, offering glimpses of a spectacular network of hoodoos and gullies, as well as a variety of interesting geological phenomena in the middle segment of the Paunsaugunt Plateau's escarpment. Check for parking restrictions at Bryce Point. You may need to start your trip at another trailhead or plan it around the time restrictions.

The grayish-brown sandstone and conglomerate, which are well exposed along the trail leading to Bryce Point, represent the conglomerate at Boat Mesa. The conglomerate itself can be distinguished from the sandstone because many black, red, or brown pebbles are cemented in its sandy matrix. Both coarse-grained sedimentary rocks are quite different in texture and composition from the limestone of the

> > > > > < < < < <

Bryce Point is the trailhead of several routes into the deeper parts of the escarpment. A boulder of pebbly sandstone and conglomerate lies perched above the badlands at Bryce Point (above). The geological phenomena to be seen along the Peekaboo Loop Trail as it winds through twisting lines of hoodoos are fascinating (left).

> > > > > < < < < <

Claron Formation which constitutes the rim elsewhere in the park. About 50 feet of this material can be seen in the cliffs immediately below the viewpoint. In addition, several large blocks of the conglomerate have broken away from the uppermost cliff and lie a short distance down the steep slope.

The view to the north from Bryce Point reveals a gentle downward flexure, a syncline, within the layers of the Claron Formation. This structure is a subtle feature of the panorama, but is evident as the rock layers are traced from the escarpment, across the Bryce Amphitheater, and eastward toward Bristlecone Point and the Sinking Ship on the northeastern horizon. Immediately to the west of the viewpoint (left, as you face north) is a deep gully leading down into the bottom of the Bryce Amphitheater. Though

The tunnel on the Peekaboo Trail cuts through the Claron Formation. Just beyond and west of the tunnel, the Bryce Point Fault interrupts the continuity of the reddish-brown limestone layers.

its displacement is difficult to see from Bryce Point, the Peekaboo Fault is located in this gully. Rock layers exposed in the escarpment to the west, across the gully, have been dropped down about 40 feet by movement along the Peekaboo Fault. The Peekaboo Fault is a normal fault, similar in age, origin, and manner of displacement, to the much larger Paunsaugunt Fault to the east.

In the east-facing wall of the escarpment west of (and slightly below) Bryce Point, a line of deep pockets and recesses have formed through dissolution of the white limestone member of the Claron Formation. Limestone is easily dissolved by water seeping along fractures or working its way along planes of layering in the stratified sequence. Gradually, this type of chemical weathering develops large cavities in the limestone. As headward erosion of the tributaries to Bryce Creek forces the escarpment to retreat to the west, the cavities are revealed as a series of recesses and archlike pockets called the Grottos. Note that these grottos are restricted to a certain level within the rock sequence exposed in the escarpment. This is because the cavities have formed within a series of layers in the Claron Formation which are composed of especially pure, and therefore very soluble, limestone. Above and below the line of grottos, the layers are composed of less soluble rock such as impure limestone, dolomitic limestone, or limy mudstone.

Bryce Point is the trailhead of several routes into the deeper parts of the escarpment. The Peekaboo Loop Trail offers a fascinating array of geological phenomena along its 5.5-mile course. The trail is moderately strenuous, but the vistas and the interesting geology are well worth the 4 or 5 hours required to make the hike. The trail leads east from Bryce Point along the rim of the escarpment to an intersection with the Hat Shop Trail, where it begins to descend through the white limestone member of the Claron Formation. Farther along the trail, beginning at a point just above the tunnel cut through a narrow fin of mottled pink and orange-brown silty limestone, the lower pink member is exposed. Immediately beyond this tunnel, the trail is bounded on the south by a wall of thick-bedded red-brown limestone. These conspicuous beds can be traced about 50 yards down the trail, where they disappear into a steep gully intersecting the footpath. This gully, as suggested by the abrupt termination of the rock layers in it, marks the trace of the Bryce Point Fault, a reverse fault which has elevated the block on its east side by about 50 feet. Walking past the ravine, look down into it to see evidence of this fracture slashing diagonally across the rock layers on your lower left. The Bryce Point Fault was developed by compressive forces millions of years before the uplift and erosion of the Paunsaugunt Plateau.

As you continue down the trail from the Bryce Point Fault, the upper rim comes into view directly above you. From this perspective, both the upper white and lower pink members of the Claron Formation can be seen in the sheer cliffs. The trail loops around the end of Bryce Point and swings southwest where you can see the Grottos and the Wall of Windows, hanging high on the cliffs along

Bryce Point Fault is visible in the deep gully just west of the tunnel on the upper Peekaboo Trail. The eastern block has moved up by about 50 feet along this reverse fault (left).

The dissolution of limestone forms pockets and cavities in the strata of the Claron Formation. When a narrow fin of limestone develops from the erosion of the two adjacent canyons, the cavities are transformed into "windows" piercing the wall of rock. The Wall of Windows (above) is visible along the Peekaboo Trail.

Beyond the sculpted hoodoos, the Peekaboo Fault cuts through the rocks of the Claron Formation forming the escarpment above the Peekaboo Trail. The small displacement along this fault is sometimes difficult to see. Only the mismatched bands of color in the upper cliffs show the offset.

the western margin of the Bryce Amphitheater. Eventually, the path joins with the Peekaboo Loop, and after a 3-mile journey to the bottom of Bryce Creek, you can connect with several other trails or, return to Bryce Point. The Peekaboo Fault, a minor normal fault, passes very near the intersection of the trail to Bryce Point and the Peekaboo Loop Trail. The deep gully leading up to the rim southeast of the trail junction marks the actual trace of the fault. In the upper head of this gully, some displacement of the rock layers can usually be detected by carefully scrutinizing the exposures below the rim.

From this intersection, the Peekaboo Loop leads southward and down to the floor of an unnamed tributary of Bryce Creek. Erosion of the shattered rock along the Peekaboo Fault has deepened this canyon. From the point where the trail crosses the usually dry streambed, look directly upstream to see the white walls of the southern rim where a deep cleft marks the trace of the fault. Continuing its descent into the Bryce Amphitheater, the trail passes a horse corral, leaves the main gully, and winds back up the slope beneath the Wall of Windows and the Grottos. Spectacular hoodoos line the trail for a considerable distance in this portion of the Peekaboo Loop, Note that the hoodoos here are developed in the lower pink member of the Claron Formation, where mixed rock types and relatively impure limestones intensify the effects of differential erosion to produce a varied array of peculiar landforms. Above, the pure limestone of the white member, in which the Grottos have developed in the sheer cliffs, weathers at a more uniform rate.

The trail climbs to a tunnel which opens above yet another bowl filled with magnificent stone pinnacles. These hoodoos have been formed by the headward erosion of another small tributary to Bryce Creek. The Bryce Amphitheater is comprised of several such small erosional bowls consolidated into a large basin. Approximately half a mile farther down the trail, the main channel of Bryce Creek comes into view. The trail descends gradually toward the bottom of the canyon through the smooth slopes which, for the most part, conceal the outcrops of the Wahweap Formation. Near the bottom of the canyon, it connects with the path leading back to Bryce Point. As the trail ascends back to the rim, it swings past several large boulders of gray, white, and pink limestone of the Claron Formation. As you pass these boulders, pause to examine closely the color, layering, fossils, and surface texture of these rocks. You will gain an appreciation for the variety of sediment which accumulated on the floor of Flagstaff Lake more than 50 million years ago.

SUNSET POINT
AND THE NAVAJO LOOP TRAIL

Sunset Point overlooks the Silent City, one of the most spectacular fields of hoodoos anywhere in the park. These erosional landforms literally fill the broad bowl of the Bryce Amphitheater, below and to the south of Sunset Point. The hoodoos here are developed in the pink limestone member of the Claron Formation and are the product of the headward erosion of Bryce Creek, a primary tributary to the Paria River. Southwest from Sunset Point, across the upper end of the amphitheater, note that Inspiration Point is poised atop a prominent cliff of the white limestone member of the Claron Formation. From Inspiration Point south and east, you can trace these white layers continuously. They have been eroded from the area around Sunset Point, however, and the rock at your feet belongs to the lower

> > > > > < < < < <

The Wall Street canyon has been widened at the bottom as large blocks of rock adjacent to the trail have fallen inward. The hanging ceiling, composed of a thin layer of mudstone, will one day fall as well, enlarging the narrow slot overhead (above). Hoodoos in a portion of the Silent City are seen from Sunset Point (left).

> > > > > < < < < <

pink limestone member. South from Sunset Point, across the main part of the Bryce Amphitheater, is Bryce Point. The light brownish-colored rocks around this popular viewpoint are sandstone and conglomerate of the conglomerate at Boat Mesa, so named because it caps Boat Mesa to the north. It is very discontinuous in its distribution, but the small patch of it at Bryce Point can be traced for a short distance along the rim toward Inspiration Point. Immediately west of Bryce Point, note that the rim descends into a broad gully. This gully marks the position of the Peekaboo Fault, a normal fault which displaces rock layers down to the west by about 50 feet. Let your eyes drift down the gully toward the floor of the amphitheater. Look for displacement on this small fault, indicated by the offset of faintly colored layers in the

The diagonal parallel grooves etched into the rock are scour marks produced by the runoff of water along the base of the cliffs.

Claron Formation. The offset is not always easy to see, but good lighting and close scrutiny will usually reveal it. A good reference horizon to use in searching for the fault is the line of solution cavities, known as grottos, which have developed in the lower part of the white limestone of the Claron Formation. Look for the offset in this line of cavities on either side of the Peekaboo Fault.

The Navajo Loop Trail offers a convenient opportunity to become more familiar with the geologic fabric of the park. This steep hike descends to the floor of the Bryce Amphitheater and returns to Sunset Point via a 1.3-mile loop. The loop may be traveled in either direction, but if you descend into the narrow gorge known as Wall Street, you encounter a number of interesting geological phenomena immediately. Near the top of the loop, as you begin your descent, note the diagonal parallel grooves etched into the rock walls. These are scour marks produced by the runoff of water along the base of the cliffs. They indicate the location of the slope surface, prior to its erosional retreat. As you continue to descend, note that the trail winds back and forth across a steep slope consisting of the loose products of weathering. The material on this slope is continually moving downhill and sometimes is washed out over the trail, particularly after a vigorous rain. Look for signs of such downslope movement. About halfway from the rim to the entrance of Wall Street, the narrowing canyon walls are coated with dripstone, formed as water from rain and melting snow cascaded down the sheer face leaving dissolved minerals, principally

calcite, behind. This thin, but durable, coating may look like dripping candle wax, but it serves to protect the steep walls from erosion, helping them remain vertical as the slope recedes from their base.

As you enter the gloomy shade of Wall Street, examine the rock layers exposed in its walls. Alternating ledges and recesses reflect the varying abilities of individual layers in the Claron Formation to resist erosion. Once you are in the defile, note the overhanging, partially open "ceiling," which developed as a thin—and relatively weak—layer of mudstone eroded rapidly away, leaving the limestone above it unsupported. The canyon has been widened at the bottom as large blocks of rock adjacent to the trail have fallen inward. The hanging ceiling will one day fall as well, enlarging the narrow slot overhead. Eventually, these broken blocks will be flushed out of the canyon by flash floods which periodically roar through this narrow canyon. As you continue down Wall Street, look for signs of such flood-induced scouring on the uneven floor of the ravine.

When you emerge from the lower end of Wall Street, you'll be very near the bottom of the Claron Formation. In more open terrain leading toward the upper end of Bryce Creek, you'll see that the surface is covered with loose alluvium, the unconsolidated granular product of weathering. Concealed beneath this thin veneer of debris are the soft rocks of the Wahweap Formation, weakly cemented mudstone and sandstone, which weather rapidly into the smooth slopes seen along the bottom of the Bryce Amphitheater. Beginning its ascent back to Sunset Point, the Navajo Loop Trail swings into a narrow gorge cut through the Claron Formation. As you return, examine the canyon walls for patches of pebbles and cobbles, embedded in a sandy matrix, adhering to the canyon walls. This gravelly material represents ancient alluvium cemented in place by the precipitation of calcite from water flowing over the land surface. Recent downcutting in the canyon has left remnant patches of rubble resting high above the modern floor of the gorge. At the top of steep switchbacks, the trail emerges from the shaded canyon and gently rises to the rim.

Near the end of the trail, you will pass Thor's Hammer, one of the best-known landforms in the park. The large block resting atop this prominent hoodoo is a resistant cap of limestone, while the reddish material below is impure, more easily eroded, silty limestone and mudstone. Many of the most imposing hoodoos in Bryce Canyon have a similar cap, a large block balanced on top of a narrow column of softer rock. This characteristic shape of hoodoos is probably why there are so many allusions to human or animal forms in their informal names; they often appear to have "heads."

Patches of ancient alluvium cling to the canyon walls along the Navajo Loop Trail. These patches of cemented gravel were deposited by water prior to the most recent down-cutting.

111

SUNRISE POINT
AND THE QUEEN'S GARDEN TRAIL

Sunrise Point is one of four viewpoints which overlook the Bryce Amphitheater, a large embayment carved into the eastern rim of the Paunsaugunt Plateau by the headwaters of Bryce Creek. Extending east from Sunrise Point, the long ridge stretching toward Bristlecone Point separates this great bowl of erosion from the amphitheater carved by the headwaters of Campbell Creek to the north. Sunrise is also the starting point of the Queen's Garden Trail, a moderate 1.8-mile hike, which is one of the most popular footpaths in the park.

At the viewpoint, a small limber pine tree clings to the edge of the eroding cliff, its roots exposed. The rocks on which you stand here belong to the red limestone member of the Claron Formation. The overlying white limestone member has been removed by

> > > > > < < < < <

The Queen's Garden Trail leads through an especially colorful part of the Claron Formation. Retreat of the slope at Sunrise Point has exposed part of the root system under a small limber pine tree (above). The white limestone member of the Claron Formation forms the rimrock of the Bryce Amphitheater (left).

> > > > > < < < < <

erosion, but you can see it capping the rim of Bryce Amphitheater near Bryce Point to the south. Below the cliff, a spectacular tangle of hoodoos and stone walls stands above the shadowy defiles leading down to the canyon floor.

The first few steps down the Queen's Garden Trail lead through an especially colorful part of the Claron Formation. A thick layer of resistant white limestone caps many of the hoodoos here. Beneath, a poorly layered sequence of silty limestone is tinged with a lavender glow, produced by small amounts of oxidized manganese in the rock. Lower still, the rock is an impure limestone and mudstone mixture containing iron oxides, which impart a rusty hue to the shaded walls. Parallel scour marks raked across the walls in many places reveal the movement of the slope over time.

As the trail continues to descend, it cuts into the side of a low ridge and hugs a 10-foot wall of rock on the south side. Pause here and look carefully at the fractured rocks of the Claron Formation. The creamy white limestone has been thoroughly broken by frost wedging and other agents of erosion. Notice how plant roots penetrate some of the fractures from the soil above, helping to widen the cracks and hasten the disintegration of the limestone. Close examination of this limestone will reveal the smooth, even texture typical of such sedimentary rocks. Occasionally, you will see gray fragments of fossil shells in this limestone. If you are especially persistent in your observations, you may notice the ill-preserved form of a coiled snail in the limestone. These molluscs lived in the mud of an ancient lake 50 – 60 million years ago. Tiny spherical or rod-shaped objects can also been seen in this rock. These grains are called oolites because they resemble eggs. They represent calcite-coated particles rolled across the lake bottom by currents.

Farther down the trail, the layers of the Claron Formation become more variable. Near signpost 5, impure limestone is interbedded with dolomitic limestone and limy mudstone. Various rock types erode at different rates giving rise to the layered fluting on the walls of the fins and sides of the hoodoos. Softer mudstones generally form recesses or pockets between projecting ledges eroded from the more durable limestone and dolomitic limestone.

A few more minutes down the trail will bring you to an open area where soft white rocks have eroded into an undulating flat. This area, where

Bristlecone pines are particularly abundant, is littered with stones and boulders, the caprock of ancient hoodoos, now obliterated by rapid erosion of the soft substrate. In time, even the stones will disappear, and no trace will remain of the once-grand columns.

The footpath next intersects with the horse trail, curves around the nose of a ridge, and continues its descent to the Queen's Garden. Along the way, you will pass through small tunnels cut into the Claron Formation. Note the craggy dark-colored ledges projecting from walls along this part of the trail. These are dolomitic limestone layers, the most resistant of the rocks in this part of the layered succession. As you pass the rock outcrops, slide your hand over the surface of the walls and boulders along the trail. The dolomitic limestone layers will feel smooth and even-textured; other layers will feel gritty. The gritty rocks are sandstone, consisting of fine sand grains loosely cemented with calcite. The sand grains are loosely bound and the rock crumbles readily. Imagine how easily these rocks must yield to the forces of mechanical weathering.

At trail's end, as you view the many curious pinnacles in the Queen's Garden, remember that each is the ephemeral product of rock and weather. Each is changing even as you watch. The next rain will wash a few more grains away and dissolve a little more calcite. Periodically, a whole slab of stone will fall from the side or top of a hoodoo, radically changing its appearance. Eventually, all of these pillars are destined to become silt traveling along in the muddy water of the Paria River.

The ultimate fate of all hoodoos is to be reduced to a scattering of stones by the relentless attack of the agents of erosion.

FAIRYLAND CANYON
AND THE FAIRYLAND LOOP TRAIL

Fairyland Canyon, located in the northern part of the park, is one of the amphitheaters carved most recently into the edge of the Paunsaugunt Plateau. The canyon is not as deep than those incised into the higher southern parts of the plateau. The hoodoos and other erosional landforms are less developed here than in the more deeply eroded portions of the escarpment. Nonetheless, several types of faults, unique patterns of erosion, and excellent exposures of the varied rocks of the Claron Formation are all encountered in this beautiful ravine.

The Fairyland Overlook is a good place to begin a hike along the Fairyland Loop Trail, although the trail is also accessible near Sunrise Point and from any place along the rim between the two viewpoints. The loop is about 8 miles long, but is only moderately strenuous as it descends 900 feet

> > > > > < < < < <

Tower Bridge is formed from a resistant ledge of dolomitic limestone suspended between, and about halfway down, two spires of red mudstone (above). Hoodoos in Fairyland Canyon are still developing through the erosion of fins in the Claron Formation. The orange and red walls are cleaved by vertical joints (left).

> > > > > < < < < <

into Fairyland Canyon, circles Boat Mesa, climbs up through the Campbell Creek drainage to join the rim trail, and then returns to the overlook.

Fairyland Canyon is cut east from the overlook through colorful exposures of red, orange, pink, and gray rocks of the Claron Formation. The underlying Cretaceous strata are not visible even in the depths of the upper canyon because limited down-cutting in this part of the park has yet to penetrate the entire thickness of the Claron. The Cretaceous Straight Cliffs and Wahweap formations are exposed only in the lower part of the canyon near the Paunsaugunt Fault, far to the east of the rim. Boat Mesa dominates your view to the south across the upper end of the canyon as you descend by the Fairyland Trail. The light gray caprock is the conglomerate at

Boat Mesa, which rests upon the red, pink, and white strata of the Claron Formation. In the middle of the north-facing wall of Boat Mesa, a thick ledge of limestone is offset by about 20 feet along the Fairyland Fault. This small normal fault passes from north to south directly under Boat Mesa, but unlike most of the normal faults in the Paunsaugunt region, it has elevated the western block relative to the eastern block. The displacement is relatively small, but it can be detected by careful examination of the Claron strata. The conglomerate at Boat Mesa extends over these faulted red layers as a continuous sheet of hardened sand and gravel. The Fairyland Fault must therefore have been active sometime after the Claron Formation was deposited (50 – 60 million years ago), but before the sandstone and conglomerate cap accumulated (about 35 million years ago).

In the walls of rock rising from the gullies of the upper Fairyland Canyon area, several small reverse faults may be also be seen. These faults can be identified by the slight offset of rock layers along diagonal fractures across the cliff faces and the vertical walls of the columns and spires. Upper Fairyland Canyon is only about two miles south of the Ruby's Inn Thrust, the largest reverse fault in the region; it is likely that the small faults here are related to the compressive force which developed that larger structure some 20 to 40 million years ago.

As the trail proceeds down the ridge toward the lower end of Fairyland Canyon, it passes through walls and pillars eroded from a strikingly colorful part of the lower Claron Formation. The purple, red, and maroon walls here are cleaved by numerous vertical joints. Erosion along these fractures has decorated the walls with statuesque hoodoos and developed the fluted slots which penetrate down through the bedrock. At the lower end of Fairyland Canyon, the chasm opens into a wide basin encircled by towering sculpted walls eroded from the Claron Formation. Several small thrust faults can be seen in these walls if the layers are carefully examined for evidence of displacement.

After crossing Fairyland Creek, the trail swings around the east end of Boat Mesa and climbs back toward the rim. Even in this lower end of Fairyland Canyon, downcutting streams have not yet dissected the Claron Formation completely, leaving the underlying Cretaceous strata still mostly concealed. This is because the rocks in this portion of the park have only recently been affected by the headward erosion of Fairyland Creek, a tributary to the Paria River. As the streams continue to cut deeper into the edge of the Paunsaugunt Plateau, more of the Claron Formation will be removed, exposing the underlying strata and creating the grayish badlands seen at the bottom of the canyons to the south.

As the Fairyland Loop winds around the southeast side of Boat Mesa, it enters the amphitheater carved by Campbell Creek. The trail passes many interesting landforms resulting from the differential erosion of the rocks in the Claron Formation as it ascends west toward the escarpment. Tower Bridge, reached by a short side trail leaving the main path near the bottom of Campbell Canyon, is formed from a resistant ledge of dolomitic limestone suspended between, and about halfway down, two spires of red mudstone.

Crossing the rocky bed of Campbell Creek, the trail climbs up the nose of a long ridge to provide an excellent view of the Chinese Wall. Columns of rock along the wall are separated by joints which become wider near the eastern end of the ledge where well-formed hoodoos are developing in a resistant layer of white limestone. This is because the eastern end of the ledge was subjected to erosion long ago as the soft slope gradually receded west. The western portion has only recently emerged from the protective cover of overlying rocks.

The trail meets the rim again near Sunrise Point. Hikers can return to the Fairyland Overlook via the Rim Trail by following it north. This return route climbs a flat-topped point projecting toward Boat Mesa and capped by the sandstone and conglomerate which bears its name. There are many good trailside outcrops of coarse brown sandstone and light gray pebbly conglomerate along this final leg of the Fairyland Loop Trail.

As the trail proceeds down the ridge toward the lower end of Fairyland Canyon, it passes through walls and pillars eroded from a strikingly colorful part of the lower Claron Formation (left).

PHOTOGRAPHER'S NOTES

Two rather profound but opposite concepts had to be considered in making the photographs for this book. First, the rocks of Bryce Canyon record a geologic history of nearly 200 million years, an incomprehensible time span for most people. In human perception the great Earth gesture that created Bryce Canyon is changeless, unvarying and infinite. In a study of its timeless geology one would naturally think that any photographs of the stratified rock record would reveal all that is necessary to know about its ancient history and make-up. However, while these rocks are the object of our study, we must understand how they are revealed to the eye and subsequently the camera.

The second concept may be more elusive and difficult to comprehend. Photography, which literally means drawing with light, is profoundly dependant on the constantly changing quality of light. In the static two-dimensional photograph, the illusion of form, texture and depth is created by the light rather than the objects themselves. In landscape photography in general, and particularly at Bryce Canyon where the average elevation is 8,000 feet, the light is continually changing. Hence, the same hoodoo, spire, fin, or formation can be revealed to the camera as a vapid pile of rocks or a magical translucent gem, depending on the transient quality of light. So, while photographing the most stable and unchanging element on the planet—the rocks—one must understand that the rocks themselves are being illuminated and revealed by the most ephemeral and fleeting of elements—the light. The magic is contained not in the rocks alone, but in the way they are revealed by the light. The weathers, the atmosphere, the time of day and even the time of year all contribute to this quality of light, and for one to see magic in the rocks, one must know the magic of the light.

Bryce Canyon is predominantly an east-facing park. It can therefore be expected that good light will occur almost every morning near sunrise— referred to as the "sweet light." The early morning light with its low angle and warm hues bathes the canyon with pink, then yellow light that etches every detail in the formations. As the sun climbs higher in the sky, the color becomes softer, more muted, and the sense of depth and detail becomes flatter. In addition to this, the sun rises and sets at a slightly different position on the horizon each day. It rises at its northern extreme in the middle of June (June 21 is the summer solstice) and is at its southern extreme in the middle of December (December 21 is the winter solstice), with a difference of over 60° on the horizon. As a result of this, formations from a given point will have a significantly different illumination in June than they will in December.

The stirring of each new day begins nearly an hour before the sun actually rises with soft warm light spilling over the multi-colored rocks, and they seem to glow from within. The intensity grows as the lavender sky gives way to golden yellow. The view points that are crowded during the mid-day hours are mostly deserted when this spectacle of light occurs each day. The solitude is precious and finally as the sun breaks free of the eastern horizon and breathes the fullness of golden life into the rocks and canyon walls, it also warms the soul as well as the body. At over 8,000 feet, even in summer it's rather cool at sunrise.

Winter sunrises are equally amazing with the added element of crystalline blue snow that contrasts with the multi-colored Claron Formation. Winter sunrise temperatures can plummet far below zero, but the effort is still rewarding. In winter, the camera tripod, which is frequently placed on deep soft snow, is equipped with specially designed six-inch diameter discs attached to the bottom of each tripod leg to prevent camera and tripod from being swallowed in the cold drift.

Sunsets are also quite nice but not as predictable as sunrise. The shadows creep across the amphitheater in the late afternoon, creating difficult contrast problems that do not occur in the morning. But with cooperative weather, the sweet light around sunset can also be spectacular. Frequent summer thunderstorms with spectacular cloud formations and irregular patterns of light and shade sweep across the amphitheaters during the late afternoon and are usually followed by breathtaking rainbows that announce the calm ending to an emotion-filled storm. Thunderstorms are dangerous and precautions should be taken. A little while after sunset the rocks again take on a transparent glow similar to the pre-sunrise glow, which slowly gives way to the darkening sky above Bryce Canyon.

To experience both extremes of the day necessitates, of course, long working hours,

especially during the summer when sunrise is about 6:30 A.M. and sunset is after 8:30 P.M. With "glow time," that means up at 5:00 A.M. and last light between 9:00 and 9:30 P.M. Let us share yet another little secret that is referred to as "map study." During the middle of the day when the light is not very interesting, find a comfortable spot, lay on your back and hold a large map above your face. In a short while the map will be resting on your face as you sleep away the afternoon.

The most commonly asked questions about photographs include what kind of camera and film are used. In answering that, I must first stress that cameras do not take pictures — people do. The camera is merely the tool that is used. Even as owning a Steinway does not make one a pianist, owning a good camera does not guarantee great pictures. Having said that, I will share that almost all of the pictures were taken with either a Bronica GS1 (6x7-cm) camera that includes three different lenses, or a wooden Deardorff (4x5 / 5x7-inch) camera that includes six different lenses. The photographs were captured on either Kodak Ektachrome 100 Plus or Fuji Velvia, and as for exposure data, each frame was adequately exposed, anywhere from 1/125th of a second to 30 seconds. Oh yes, a tripod comes in handy too.

Good Light!

John Telford

GLOSSARY OF GEOLOGICAL TERMS

ANTICLINE. An upward fold developed in a rock sequence.

CALCITE. The most common of the carbonate minerals, consisting of calcium carbonate, $CaCO_3$. Calcite forms in a variety of geological settings, but is particularly common in limestone and as the cementing agent in other sedimentary rocks.

COMPRESSION. The reduction in length, or "squeezing" of rocks or other materials.

CONGLOMERATE. A coarse-grained sedimentary rock consisting dominantly of particles (pebbles, etc.) larger than 2-mm in size.

CREEP. The gradual downslope movement of soil and rock particles under the influence of gravity. The rate of creep depends on the angle of the slope, moisture content of the soil, and physical characteristics of the soil particles.

CRETACEOUS PERIOD. The last period of the Mesozoic Era on the geologic time scale, beginning around 144 million years ago and ending 66 million years ago.

DIFFERENTIAL EROSION. Erosion that occurs at varying rates reflecting the differences in hardness of various rocks. Softer and weaker rocks, such as mudstone, are rapidly eroded, while more resistant materials, such as limestone, deteriorate slowly.

DOLOMITE. A carbonate mineral containing calcium and magnesium with the composition of $CaMg(CO_3)$. Dolomite commonly occurs with calcite in sedimentary rocks such as limestone.

DRIPSTONE. A common term applied to calcium carbonate deposited by water trickling over a rock surface. The term arises from the driplike tapestries which result from the steady precipitation of minerals from the water.

EOCENE EPOCH. The epoch of the Tertiary Period following the Paleocene and preceding the Oligocene. The Eocene Epoch begins about 58 million years ago and ends around 37 million years ago.

EPOCH. A subdivision of a period of geologic time.

ERA. A large increment of time on the geological time scale, consisting of several periods and encompassing tens or hundreds of millions of years.

EXTENSION. The increase in length, or "stretching" of material.

EROSION. The general process of disintegration of solid rock and the removal of its products by such agents as wind, water, and gravity.

Pelecypods (bi-valve molluscs) from the early Cenozoic Era once lived in Bryce's ancient lakes.

EROSION *(continued)*

Erosion is a dynamic process which removes the debris produced by weathering.

FAULT. A fracture in the earth's crust across which there is relative movement of the rocks on either side.

FAULT PLANE. The surface of rupture in a faulted rock sequence.

FIN. A narrow wall of rock which generally develops when parallel joints or fractures on either side of it are widened through erosion, reducing the width of the standing rock.

FORMATION. A body of rock which consists dominantly of material with uniform characteristics, or with features which vary within limited ranges. In geological usage, the term is not applied to individual landforms which have peculiar shapes and forms.

FROST WEDGING. The widening and extension of fractures in rock as a consequence of the increase in volume which accompanies the freezing of water. When ice forms from water within the small fractures, it works to pry the rocks apart by forcing the cracks open.

HEADWARD EROSION. The lengthening of a stream channel or gully upstream as a result of progressive erosion of the land by running water.

HOODOO. An ornate column, spire, or tower produced by the differential erosion of bedrock. Hoodoos must often form in areas of intense, intermittent rainfall and runoff.

JOINT. A natural fracture in rock with no displacement of the adjacent blocks; a simple crack in bedrock.

LAVA. A term applied to magma which erupts on the earth's surface during volcanic events.

LIMESTONE. A generally non-granular sedimentary rock composed primarily of calcium carbonate in the form of the mineral calcite, $CaCO_3$.

MAGMA. The hot fluid generated beneath the earth's surface from which igneous rocks form after cooling and solidification. Magma is essentially molten rock, but may also contain dissolved gases and fragments of solid material.

MEMBER. A subdivision of a formation; a body of rock with characteristics embraced by the definition of the formation, but distinctive from other members within it.

MUDSTONE. A granular sedimentary rock, generally blocky or massive, composed of roughly equal amounts of clay and silt or fine sand.

Fossil remains of birch leaves suggest a cool temperate climate with moderate precipitation that once characterized the Bryce Canyon region. Birch species evolved in the late Mesozoic Era, around 130 million years ago, and have been a common form ever since.

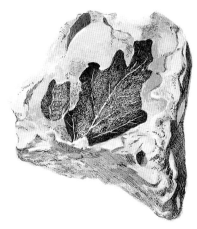

NORMAL FAULT. A fault which forms by the extension of the earth's crust, characterized by downward movement of the block above the fault plane.

OLIGOCENE EPOCH. An epoch of the Tertiary following the Eocene, extending from approximately 37 million to 24 million years ago.

OROGENY. A mountain-building event; a period of deformation which results in the development of a mountain system.

OXIDATION. The combination of oxygen with one of the metallic elements, such as iron or manganese. Oxidized materials, such as hematite, an iron oxide, form through this style of chemical weathering.

PALEOCENE EPOCH. The first epoch of the Tertiary Period, beginning about 66 million years ago and concluding around 58 million years ago.

PEDOGENESIS. The formation of soil through the combined action of biological, chemical, and physical weathering.

PERIOD. One of the principal units of the geologic time scale, ranging in duration from about 70 million years to less than 2 million years. The various unequal periods are grouped into larger time intervals known as eras, and subdivided into smaller epochs.

PLATEAU. A comparatively flattopped landform which rises well above the lower terrain around it. In general, plateaus are broader than they are high and are usually bounded by cliffs or steep slopes which descend to lower terrain. Plateaus often form where the underlying rock is horizontally stratified, but this is not always the case.

PRECIPITATION. In a geological context, the formation of solid minerals from the chemicals dissolved in water. Calcite ($CaCO_3$), for example, is precipitated from water when the calcium, carbon, and oxygen atoms combine in a regular geometric array. The formation of crystals of "rock candy" from a solution of sugar and water is a common example of precipitation.

REVERSE FAULT. A fault, formed by the compression of rock, in which the block above the fault plane moves up relative to the block below.

SAND. A fragment or particle of rock having a diameter between 2-mm and 1/16-mm.

SANDSTONE. A granular sedimentary rock composed of compacted and cemented grains of sand between 2-mm and 1/16-mm in size.

SHALE. A very fine-textured sedimentary rock consisting of particles less than 1/256-mm (microscopic) in size.

This mammoth jaw fragment may be more than 20,000 years old. It was found in the park in 1967. Woolly mammoths adapted well to the frigid temperatures of the ice ages.

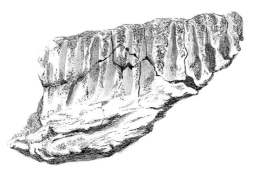

SILT. A fragment or particle having a diameter between 1/256- and 1/16-mm; accumulations of silt have a gritty texture.

SILTSTONE. A granular sedimentary rock composed of compacted and cemented silt grains.

SLAB FAILURE. The collapse of a tabular block of rock, separated from unweathered bedrock by joints, from a vertical cliff. The slabs detached by this process may fall suddenly or slide gradually to the slopes below the cliff.

SLICKENSIDE. A smooth, scratched, and sometimes polished surface produced by the opposed movement of blocks of rock on either side of a fault plane.

SOIL. The unconsolidated material present at the earth's surface which covers unweathered bedrock. Soil consists of the granular and chemical products of weathering and contains varying amounts of organic material such as plant roots and insects.

STRIATION. A linear groove or scratch on a rock surface. Striations generally occur in sets of parallel grooves reflecting the movement of one mass against another. Striated rock surfaces can be produced by glaciers, faults, and rockslides.

SYNCLINE. A downward fold developed in a sequence of rock.

TERTIARY PERIOD. The first period of the Cenozoic Era of the geological time scale. Encompasses the interval from about 66 million years ago to approximately 1.8 million years ago.

THRUST FAULT, THRUST. A fault characterized by the upward movement of the block above a fault plane inclined at an angle of less than 45 degrees. Thrust faults form by compression of rock masses.

TREND. A general term for the direction or bearing of a geologic feature or a linear landform such as a mountain range or valley.

UNCONFORMITY. A "gap" in a rock sequence; a plane within a succession of rock layers which represents an interval of time during which no rocks formed. Unconformities are generally marked by an undulating surface separating the layers above and below. The strata above and below sometimes meet at an angle along the unconformity, in which case it is known as an angular unconformity.

WEATHERING. The spontaneous changes in rock which result from exposure to the physical conditions at the earth's surface, with little or no transport of the loose products. Weathering refers to both the physical disintegration and chemical deterioration of solid rock. Erosion differs from weathering in that it includes processes which both produce and transport the products of rock corrosion.

This fossilized dinosaur bone of an unknown species dates from the late Mesozoic, 135 to 65 million years ago, when this region had a warm, moist climate.

This fossil ammonite shell, from Paria Creek near the park, is similar to that of today's Pearly Nautilus. The ammonite has been extinct for roughly 70 million years.

BIBLIOGRAPHY

ANDERSON, J. J., and P. D. ROWLEY. 1975. Cenozoic stratigraphy of southwestern High Plateaus of Utah. Boulder, CO: Geological Society of America Special Paper 160.

BOWERS, W. E. 1972. The Canaan Peak, Pine Hollow, and Wasatch formations in the Table Cliffs region, Garfield County, Utah. Washington, D.C., G.P.O: U.S. Geological Survey Bulletin 1331-B.

BOWERS, W. E. 1991. Geologic map of Bryce Canyon National Park and vicinity, southwestern Utah, 1:24000. Washington, D.C., G.P.O: U.S. Geological Survey map I-2108.

BROX, G. S. 1961. The geology and erosional development of northern Bryce Canyon National Park. Master's thesis, University of Utah, Salt Lake City.

DAVIS, G. H., and R. W. KRANZ. 1986. Post "Laramide" thrusting in the Claron Formation, Bryce Canyon National Park, Utah. Geological Society of America Abstracts with Programs 18: 98.

DOELLING, H. H. 1975. Geology and mineral resources of Garfield County, Utah. Salt Lake City, Utah: Utah Geological and Mineral Survey Bulletin 107.

DUTTON, C. E. 1880. Report on the Geology of the High Plateaus of Utah. U.S. Geographical and Geological Survey Rocky Mountain Region Report.

EATON, J. G., and R. L. CIFELLI. 1988. Preliminary report on Late Cretaceous mammals of the Kaiparowits Plateau, southern Utah. Contributions to Geology, University of Wyoming (Laramie) 26 (no.2): 45 – 55.

GREGORY, H. E. 1949. Geologic and geographic reconnaissance of the eastern Markagunt Plateau. Geological Society of America Bulletin 60: 969 – 98.

GREGORY, H. E. 1951. The geology and geography of the Paunsaugunt region, Utah. U.S. Geological Survey Professional Paper 226.

GREGORY, H. E., and R. C. MOORE. 1931. The Kaiparowits region, a geographic and geologic reconnaissance of parts of Utah and Arizona. U.S. Geological Survey Professional Paper 164.

HOWELL, E. E. 1875. Report on the geology of portions of Utah, Nevada, Arizona, and New Mexico. U.S. Geographical and Geological Survey West of 100th Meridian (Wheeler survey) 3: 227 – 301.

HUNT, C. B. 1956. Cenozoic geology of the Colorado Plateau. U.S. Geological Survey Professional Paper 279.

LINDQUIST, R. C. 1977. The geology of Bryce Canyon National Park. Bryce Canyon, UT: Bryce Canyon Natural History Association.

LINDQUIST, R. C. 1980. Slope processes and forms at Bryce Canyon National Park. Ph.D. Dissertation, University of Utah, Salt Lake City.

LUNDIN, E. R. 1989. Thrusting of the Claron Formation, the Bryce Canyon region, Utah. Geological Society of America Bulletin 101: 1050 – 83.

MULLET, D. J., N. A. WELLS, and J. J. ANDERSON. 1988. Early Cenozoic deposition in the Cedar-Bryce depocenter: Certainties, uncertainties, and comparison with the Flagstaff-Green River basins. Geological Society of America Abstracts with Programs 20 (no. 3): 217.

ROWLEY, P. D., J. J. ANDERSON, and P. L. WILLIAMS. 1975. A summary of Tertiary volcanic stratigraphy of the southwestern High Plateaus and adjacent Great Basin, Utah. U.S. Geological Survey Bulletin 1405-B: B1 – B20.

ROWLEY, P. D., J. J. ANDERSON, P. L. WILLIAMS, and R. J. FLECK. 1978. Age of structural differentiation between the Colorado Plateau and Basin and Ranges provinces of southwestern Utah. Geology 6: 51 – 5.

ROWLEY, P. D., T. A. STEVEN, J. J. ANDERSON, and C. G. CUNNINGHAM. 1979. Cenozoic stratigraphic and structural framework of southwestern Utah. Washington, D.C., G.P.O.: U.S. Geological Survey Professional Paper 1149.

SCHNEIDER, M. C. 1967. Early Tertiary continental sediments of central and south-central Utah. Brigham Young University Geology Studies (Provo, Utah) 14: 143 – 94.

Frank De Courten

John Telford

Hannah Hinchman

Lee Riddell

FRANK DECOURTEN

Frank was educated at the University of California, Riverside and has been teaching geology and paleontology for over 16 years. His primary research interest is directed toward the Mesozoic rocks and fossils of south-central Utah. An experienced field and classroom instructor, Frank has taught at California State University, Chico, the University of Utah, and currently at Sierra College in Rocklin, California. In 1982 he received the Outstanding Teaching Award from the Department of Geology and Geophysics at the University of Utah. Frank has conducted numerous field programs for the Utah Museum of Natural History, National Wildlife Federation, Audubon Society, and other organizations.

JOHN TELFORD

John is a native of Utah and has been making photographs of the landscape and environment for nearly 25 years. His photographs have been included in *Utah Canyon Country, Blessed By Light, Visions of the Colorado Plateau,* and many other books. In 1979 Telford published *The Great Salt Lake Portfolio,* with a forward by Pulitzer Prize winner Wallace Stegner. *Coyote's Canyon* (photographs by John Telford, stories by Terry Tempest Williams) was published in 1988 by Peregrine Smith Books. *Lake Powell: A Different Light,* was released in 1994. John holds an MFA from the University of Utah and is currently an Assistant Professor in the Design Department at Brigham Young University. He and his wife Valerie have five children.

HANNAH HINCHMAN

Hannah is an illustrator and calligrapher who lives in Dubois, Wyoming. Her book, *A Life in Hand: Creating the Illuminated Journal,* was published by Peregrine Smith in 1991. Her illustrations may be seen in *Sky's Witness* by C.L. Rawlins, and one of her essays was included in *Sisters of the Earth,* edited by Lorraine Anderson. In 1994 Hannah received a Literary Fellowship from the Wyoming Arts Council. She writes and illustrates a column for *Sierra* magazine about art and natural history, and in the summer she may be found teaching courses on natural history journal keeping around the Yellowstone ecosystem, in Utah, and in Idaho. Hannah is working on a book about Wyoming's Wind River country.

LEE RIDDELL

Lee's background is in environmental education, having studied at Utah State University in Logan, Utah. Her design work reflects her love of natural history, art and the landscape, and is her way of teaching people about the things she loves. She has designed publications for many national park natural history associations across the country including Alaska, Big Bend, Bryce Canyon, Craters of the Moon, Great Smoky Mountains, Grand Teton, Yosemite and Zion. Other books include *Images of Nature: The Photographs of Thomas D. Mangelsen, Splendors of the Seas: The Photographs of Norbert Wu,* and *A Life In Hand* mentioned above. She and her husband Ed live in Jackson Hole, Wyoming, where they own an advertising, design, and photography business.